RESURRECTION

The BIG Picture of God's Purpose and Your Destiny

Allen Paul Weaver III, M. Div.

Revised & Updated Second Edition

ISBN 978-1-7360972-0-5 Paperback—Revised & Updated Second Edition

Resurrection - First Edition - © 2019

Published by: Radiant City Studios, LLC

Cover layout and design created by Allen Paul Weaver III

Books may be ordered by contacting: Allen Paul Weaver III at www.APW3.com

DEDICATION

To Jesus the Christ...

The Son of Man of Daniel 7. The Eternal Son of God. Second in the Triune Godhead. King of Kings. Lord of Lords.

Alpha and Omega—the Beginning and the End. The Living Word. The Lamb of God who takes away the sin of the world. The Son of Man who is Savior, King and Judge of humanity and all creation. The Center of all existence. The One who holds all things together. The Bright and Morning Star. The Firstborn among many brothers and sisters...

My King. My Lord. My Savior. My Friend. I am in love with you as you continue to unfold the wrappings of your love for me.

Thank you for life! Thank you for existence in this day and time! Thank you for giving me parents who helped point the way to you. Thank you for salvation, your indwelling Holy Spirit, and for blessing me with gifts and a calling to serve.

Thank you for making me a part of your eternal family and for sisters and brothers in Christ to take this journey with. Thank you for being loving, patient, kind, forgiving, compassionate, corrective, strong, humorous, and powerful!

Thank you for meeting me when I was that curious 10-year-old little boy, that scared and suicidal 17-year-old young man, that older guy at 30 who had hit his mid-life crisis, and me now in my 40's who finally realizes you are deserving of the preeminence in all things—no matter the outcome. You truly are the only way to the Father!

This book is dedicated to you. May it reach those you have deemed it to reach and draw them closer to you. In your name I pray. Amen.

CONTENTS

READ THIS FIRST

AUTHOR'S NOTICE OF INTENT

GOD HAS GIVEN US A MOST WONDERFUL GIFT CALLED IMAGINATION. With it we form mental images that allow us to see the unseen and to visualize people, places, and things. By using imagination when we read and write, we soar with characters, walk in other people's shoes, and visit other worlds—real and fictionalized.

Regrettably, we often leave our imagination tucked away when we read the Bible. Rarely do we apply this gift to ultimate reality. Often what we "see" when we read are words on the page of a "dusty old book" and nothing more.

But, there is a sweeping landscape in the Story God wants us to know. It is a Story which spans time, space, and beyond. It is the true Story about who we are, why we were created, how we ended up here, and where God desires to take us. And this Story can be overlooked if we allow ourselves to become distracted by the busyness of life.

What you hold in your hands is my attempt to creatively combine the Bible with imagination in order to paint the grand picture God has revealed to this world.

I know this attempt to "connect the dots" of Scripture may not be acceptable to everyone, for even within Christianity there are denominations which hold differing interpretations of the Scriptures. However, most of us share the core beliefs about God's trinitarian nature, Jesus being the Son of God, the fallen nature of humanity, the need of Christ as our Savior, and the fact that one day Jesus will physically return to earth as the rightful judge and king of all. In fact, did you know that 30% of the Bible is prophecy? Books like Isaiah, Ezekiel, Daniel and Revelation speak in great detail concerning our past, present and future—relaying critical information about the end times in which we live and the 2nd Coming of Jesus Christ!

This book is not meant to replace the Bible. It is also not an in-depth detailed telling of every account in the Bible. But it can serve as a fresh vantage point from which to dive into the Holy Scriptures. This book seeks to be biblically accurate, visually descriptive, and creatively plausible. It is specially formatted to help you follow God's Story.

Passages straight from Scripture are in regular black type even if they are written dramatically. However, those sections used to *"connect the dots"* on what Scripture *may imply*, and those passages where dialogue has been creatively inserted to *serve the Story*, are in *italics—and begin and end with this symbol:* **[]**. Also, as part of the formatting, you will find reference numbers throughout. These numbers correlate with a list of Scriptures at the end of the book in the Appendix for further study. You will also find additional resources in the Appendix to help you engage with God and the Bible on a deeper level.

You may find things in this book you do not agree with, never knew or never considered. But, if reading this work provokes you to ask deep questions and engage in serious Bilbe study and discussions about life, death, and what happens after we die, then it has served its purpose. May God's Spirit bless your imagination and lead you to the truth found in Jesus Christ. After all, Jesus said the Bible is all about him *(Luke 24:1-27)*.

Revised & Updated 2nd Edition Notice:

It's been a year and a half between the original release of *Resurrection* and this revised second edition. Within this time, I have continued to study the Bible as it relates to the end times and the return of Christ. As a result, I felt it necessary to publish this second edition which expands on certain areas of this book's writing and includes information on Jesus' Millennial Reign. This is central to the biblical story and yet is either misunderstood or ignored by many. It was omitted in the first edition due to my own lack of understanding. However, God graciously led me to numerous Scritpures and teachings concerning this event. I pray that the included and updated articles in the Appendix will prove helpful to you.

- Allen Paul Weaver III, M. Div.

FOREWARD

JOB IS THE FIRST PERSON TO RAISE THE QUESTION: *"If a man dies shall he live again?"* (Job 14:14). From that day humanity struggles with death and the hope that lies beyond death. No one understands why we struggle with death and the hope that death is not the end of human existence! Throughout the Bible we are presented with the prospect of the possibility that there is a resurrection of the human body *after* it has experienced death.

Jesus comes along and confirms our hopes when He said, ***"I am the resurrection and the life. The one who believes in me will live, even though they die; and whoever lives by believing in me will never die."*** (John 11:25).

Let the words of Jesus sink in for a moment...

The masses of humanity find it hard to believe and accept that we were created to live forever, however *not in our present form.* This prospect of the resurrection of the human body reveals the deep struggle we have in dealing with the reality of being mere mortals. In truth, no one wants to die and therefore there are those within the church who cling to the words of Jesus as they live in the hope of escaping the horrors of death through being resurrected.

The author of this book presents an interesting and provocative challenge to the church to re-imagine the concept of resurrection so that it is easily embraced. God blessed us with an imagination to question everything around us. It is when we use this power, coupled with the knowledge of the Holy Writ that we can see beyond our human eyes and learn to live and operate in the realm of faith.

I encourage every believer who reads this book to allow your minds to rise above the mundane. You can soar with the author to heights beyond your imagination. If you do, you will never be the same. You will look upon the resurrection with new eyes as your understanding of the Gospel deepens, along with the hope you have in Christ Jesus.

This book is an eye opener for those who are straddling the fence and for those who have planted their hopes in the truth of the Gospel of Jesus Christ.

—Allen Paul Weaver, Jr, D.Min
Senior Pastor, Bethesda Baptist Church of New Rochelle

INTRODUCTION

"If we find ourselves with a desire which nothing in this world can satisfy, the most probable explanation is that we were made for another world." **- C.S. Lewis, British Novelist, Christian Apologist**

I FIND IT INTERESTING THAT MOST OF US DON'T BAT AN EYE WHEN SCIENTISTS AND FUTURISTS TALK ABOUT HUMANITY'S PURSUIT OF LIFE AFTER DEATH, BY WAY OF TECHNOLOGY. We spend millions of dollars each year on medicines to extend our lifespans and spend even more on cryogenic equipment to preserve the human body after death, until a future time when we can be revived by advanced technology. Billions are also being spent on ways to circumvent death altogether by merging human and machine. This is called Transhumanism. One such method being pursued is the digitizing of the human brain in order to transplant a person's mind into another body, whether human or machine. It would seem that science and technology are catching up to science fiction, all in a quest for resurrection and immortality. Yet, dare to suggest that an all-powerful, triune God created us and will resurrect us to life eternal, at a future point in history *after* we physically die, and many will scoff at the idea.

But where does the longing for youth and eternal life come from? We all want to live forever. No one *really* desires to die—unless they are facing overwhelmingly painful and debilitating adversity. However, is it possible that the human race was created to live forever, but somewhere in the distant past something went horribly wrong? And what about our longing for utopia? Every culture on the planet seeks peace and prosperity in their own way, yet turmoil and conflict continually frustrate our best efforts. Where does this longing for a *better future* come from?

I believe the best explanation to these questions is found in the Bible. Now, you may be thinking, "The Bible is an ancient book!" However, *old does not mean irrelevant.* We are not random accidents of an indifferent universe. Quite the contrary; it is the purpose of the universe to birth each one of us into the Presence of God. And everything about this purpose and our longings for immortality and utopia hinges on the following truth:

"For if the dead are not raised, then Christ has not been raised either. And if Christ has not been raised, your faith is futile; you are still in your sins. Then those also who have fallen asleep in Christ are lost. If only for this life we have hope in Christ, we are of all people most to be pitied. But Christ has indeed been raised from the dead, the first fruits of those who have fallen asleep. For since death came through a man, the resurrection of the dead comes also through a man. For as in Adam all die, so in Christ all will be made alive. But each in turn: Christ, the first fruits; then, when he comes, those who belong to him. Then the end will come, when he hands over the kingdom to God the Father after he has destroyed all dominion, authority and power. For he must reign until he has put all his enemies under his feet. The last enemy to be destroyed is death."

- I Corinthians 15: 16-26

We were created to live forever! The Bible declares that our ability to do so revolves around the person of Jesus Christ, God's Son.[1] He created the world and holds the universe together by his own power.[2] If that wasn't amazing enough, he also wrapped himself in human flesh and lived among us—ultimately sacrificing his life to save us from the power of evil, sin, death and hell.[3] The Bible also declares that "God was in Christ, reconciling the world to himself."[4] The purpose of this reconciliation is to destroy the works of evil, restore a broken relationship, and to give us an eternal future where we can live forever with God.[5] Doesn't this sound like the answer to our longing for life and paradise?

The stark truth is that we are born into a world at war. Look around and you know it's true. Our neighborhoods. Our nation. Our world. Even closer to home is the mirror in our bathroom. For it reflects that we are at war within our own selves as well.[6] But what if the wars we are trying to fight go deeper than cultural, racial, gender, socio-economic, and religious differences? What if the wars we fight are just symptoms of a far deeper reality? What if *that* reality encompasses not just our world, but the entire universe?

The Bible declares that we were created as God's image bearers, but an enemy has come to destroy us. *That enemy* is not an impersonal force, but the very personification of evil: Lucifer—otherwise known as the devil.[7] This is an enemy which existed before time began and who has railed against God's Divine Order in every way possible. The result has been our death and separation from the One who has created us. But God, in his love for humanity, has come to do what we could not do for ourselves: redeem us. This is the reason for this book.

RESURRECTION seeks to reveal the big picture about God's purpose for creation and how we each have been given the gift of an amazing destiny! RESURRECTION is written in a narrative form, which pulls from the Scriptures, while using creative license to craft dialogue, descriptions, and events, which are *inferred by* the Scriptures. The result is a story which "connects the dots" to help foster a better understanding of what God is up to and how we fit into his overall plan for humanity, the world, the universe and beyond…

"The primary reality of the universe is not mass and energy at all… it is Spirit. Mass and energy is a derivative." *- Dr. John Lennox, Professor of Mathematics, Oxford University*

What if God made the universe *for* us, and the Earth was meant to be our playground? Does this possibility seem too good to be true? Some may say, "How arrogant to think the universe was made for us!" Yet, others may say, "How humbling to know God has done this." But is this question too far-fetched? Consider a baby girl born into a family, which possesses great wealth. This child didn't ask to be born. Her birth was the result of the love of the parents. She would grow, travel and experience the world. She would always have food and shelter. Still, she may never fully grasp the extent of her parents' wealth.

God is our lavish parent—a Heavenly Father who created the universe intentionally to populate this planet with human life.[8] God's wealth, wisdom, and power know no limits. And he desires to share a relationship with us, not out of loneliness, but out of an amazing love! But before that can happen, there must be a resurrection!

DEFINING RESURRECTION

The Greek word for "Resurrection" is *Anastasis*. According to Strong's Concordance of the Bible, *Anastasis* means: *rising to life; returning to life after death, usually referring to the raising to life of Jesus Christ. Being raised to life again. The base meaning of the word is the act of rising from a prone or sitting position to a standing position.*

So, what does this tell us? In the most dramatic of terms, resurrection is the complete reversal of death at the physical and supernatural level! It is the revitalization, renewal, and regeneration of every cell in your body that has decayed and atrophied beyond the point of no return. If there were a word beyond "nuclear" in its description of God's explosive power to completely transform your life—resurrection would be it!

Resurrection is a bursting forth! It is where God supernaturally infuses his abundant, overflowing and unquenchable Holy Spirit through the very atoms that make up your body; through the very substance of nature and spirit, which makes up the totality of who you are! And by this infusion God reverses what is otherwise irreversible! As we are told in 1 Corinthians 15:42-44, our natural bodies will perish in weakness, but will be raised "as something completely other" in glory, strength and immortality! Resurrection is violent—not in the sense of destruction that leads to death—but in the sense of an overflowing ability to flood death with such a torrent of raging life, that every aspect, particle, and avenue, which causes death, is wiped away!

Resurrection is not only restoring what was lost—imagine yourself in the prime of your life where you were your strongest, smartest and felt most alive—*it is also the bestowing upon us what we never had.*

I think this bears repeating: *Resurrection is not only restoring what was lost... it is also the bestowing upon us what we never had.*

Take a few moments and let these words sink in...

We see this in the imagery of rising from a prone (prostrate, lying down) position to standing upright. Our current existence on earth—no matter how strong, intelligent and vibrant we are—is restricted to a "lying down" or "sitting" position. We live under the consequences of the fall and the curse. But when Christ resurrects us with **his** life, we will be standing up completely under a power and presence we have never fully known before!

In John 11:25-26, Jesus declares to Martha before raising her brother Lazarus from the dead, *"I am the resurrection and the life. The one who believes in me will live, even though they die; and whoever lives by believing in me will never die. Do you believe this?"*

Resurrection isn't just a power that Jesus possesses. Resurrection **is** Jesus Christ! To partake of "it" is to partake of him! To partake of him is to be consumed and overtaken by "it". Resurrection is being found in Christ and him being found in you. Not in some metaphorical sense, but in actuality. There are certain aspects of resurrection we can experience now—such as the transformation that happens when we are born again, as well as the process described, in Romans 8, of being conformed into the image of Christ. However, the fullness of Christ's resurrection power will be revealed when we finally stand before him on *That Day*.

But what is Christ resurrecting us for? *(I seek to answer this question within the pages of this book.)* We won't be raised up to live in a void. Our resurrection is intricately connected to the restoration of the earth and the universe in order to fulfill God's original intent for creation! Yet, even with these defining parameters I have just provided, resurrection is actually beyond human definition, because what it truly is, we have never experienced before. Even so, I do enjoy using my imagination in conjunction with the Scriptures to picture it to the best of my ability. And I look forward to the day and the *forever after* when I will experience resurrection with my sisters and brothers in Christ!

A CENTRAL HOPE

God wants to make us new creations through his Son.[9] Jesus Christ is the central figure of the Bible and all human history![10] This is the overarching story that the Bible is telling. Yet, many of us who attend church regularly don't have a basic understanding of this fact. We can't articulate with any depth, *who Jesus is, why he came, and why it matters.* My hope is that this book will help you understand these questions and apply those answers to every area of your life.

I don't know where this book will go or who it will touch. But it is a labor of love for God's glory and for your good. The Story of the Bible is more real than the stories of our lives. My prayer is that the reality it presents will impact you in such a way that you will realize that to be heavenly minded *can* be for earthly good. In fact, Jesus was able to accomplish everything he did because the Kingdom of God was extremely real to him! May you live for God's pleasure. And may Philippians 3: 10-12 become your deepest desire...

"[10]I want to know Christ—yes, to know the power of his resurrection and participation in his sufferings, becoming like him in his death, [11]and so, somehow, attaining to the resurrection from the dead. [12]Not that I have already obtained all this, or have already arrived at my goal, but I press on to take hold of that for which Christ Jesus took hold of me."

A beautiful destiny awaits those of us who believe!

-Allen Paul Weaver III, M. Div.

PART ONE

ORIGINS...

SOMETIMES... THINGS ARE NOT AS THEY SEEM.

Golgotha. A hillside in the Middle East. Its face resembling that of a human skull. It is a place of torture and death. Here Roman soldiers stand at the ready as three men hang on three crosses. This type of death is called crucifixion, and it is seen as the ultimate sign of failure, humiliation, degradation and shame. The sun shines fiercely as a large crowd hurls insults towards the man in the middle, the one who hangs between two thieves. The thieves are paying for their crimes. The one in the center of the commotion is paying for the sin of the world—the crimes of all humanity.[11] How this is possible is no less than the greatest mystery of all...

It may be difficult to understand and even accept, but this one who is central to our story is not just a man. He is, in fact, the physical image of the invisible God—Immanuel—God with us. He is the firstborn over all creation. By him all things in the universe were created, visible and invisible... including us. All was created through him and for his pleasure, that he would have the preeminence. And now, here he is willingly laying down his life.[12]

But that is only part of the mystery. Another aspect of the mystery is the reason **WHY** he came: Sin and his love for sinners. *What kind of evil was so infiltrating, so terrible, so destructive, so incomprehensible in horror and scope to the human race that God had to come in the flesh to deliver this decisive blow?* How had evil so consumed and corrupted humanity and all the earth that the Son of God had to suffer in the place of every human who ever lived and who will ever live?[13] And soon, this one called Jesus of Nazareth would die for all. But how did we get to this point? First, we must go back to the beginning of time...

ΑΩ

Countless millennia ago... before time began, God: The Triune-Eternally-Existing-All-Powerful-All-Knowing-All-Present-One, chose to create the universe. In an instant, from a pinpoint powered by God's will, it burst forth! From God's Spirit, all matter and energy flowed as the universe began to take shape. The elements on the periodic table were forged as the fundamental forces of the cosmos began to equalize.

Then, God placed his attention on our planet, Earth. With intention, God's Spirit hovered over the depths of the water, which covered the entire surface of the planet. How long did God's Spirit linger there? No one knows. But then... God spoke! With each command reality took shape: Light... Atmosphere... Dry land and oceans... Trees and vegetation... Sun, moon, and stars... Aquatic creatures and birds... Land animals and insects.... God was pleased with what he had created.

Later, somewhere on the continent of Africa, God made humans, the epitome of his creation. This race of beings were the very crown of his handiwork. It was they who bore his distinctive imprint because he created them in his own image. The first—a man named Adam—was created from the very molecules of dust, yet imbued with the very breath of God. The second—a woman—was created in the very first surgery, when God took DNA from Adam and crafted... Eve. These two were unique in the entire universe. They were the embodiment of God's intended purpose: where the realms of heaven and earth would exist together as one expansive kingdom.

One of God's greatest gifts to humans was free will: the ability to make decisions, and ultimately to succeed and to fail. God did not want automatons—those forced or "programmed" to do God's will. God wanted beings who would live and exist within a relationship built on love and trust. Free will granted the ability to love and trust; and the possibility of breaking those ideals...

These first two humans walked with God daily in a garden paradise that was designed for them to manage. God gave them a decree to rule over the entire planet and all life which existed on it. They were to enact God's will and kingdom on earth. God also gave them one rule: they could eat from any tree in the garden except for one. The forbidden tree at the center of the garden—the tree of the knowledge of Good and Evil. If they ever chose to eat the forbidden fruit; they would be cut off from God's life-giving presence and the process of death would strike them.[14]

But what does death mean to beings created to live forever? Apparently, death had already existed, but it could only be ushered into humanity, the world, and ultimately the universe through the direct disregard of God's law. But there was a problem which stretches back even further into the past... to a *time* before time began.

ΑΩ

Heaven: The indescribable realm beyond time and space where God dwells. A place boundless in glory and unhindered by geographic constraints. In this ancient past, well before the universe existed, God created a race of angels to serve him. These beings were indescribable in their power and ability. They, too, had free will and gladly carried out their duties in realms and dimensions unimagined by human minds. They were present at the creation of the universe—a new realm seemingly infinite in scope yet given clear boundaries—and they witnessed God's wonder and handiwork as new life forms were created on a solitary planet near a yellow star.[14.1] It seems that God, always the consummate creator, was embarking upon a new experiment.

Among the angels was a ruling class. These *Archangels* stood in the very presence of God and were given special assignments that varied from the rest. Chief among the angels was Lucifer: the anointed cherub and most radiant of them all. Central to his purpose was leading the vast host of angels in worship to God, the giver and sustainer of all life and reality. How the following events happened is unclear, but at some point something shifted within Lucifer and he decided that serving God was no longer enough. Instead, Lucifer wanted to *be* God. As he rehearsed that desire *within* himself, his very nature changed as he became the originator and personification of evil in all of the realms of God. Soon, he approached the other angels. So subversive was Lucifer's words that a third of them were seduced to the dark side.[14.2]

ΑΩ

❏ *Floating mountains hover in the distance as light bounces off an angel zooming in between them. Lucifer soars from the sky on the far side of the mountain range and lands in front of myriads of angels.*

All have been given glory and power, but none on the scale and magnitude of Lucifer, the Morning Star. He is the highest-ranking cherubim in the heavenly realm—the crown of God's angelic creation. Flawless and fearless. Beautiful beyond belief. Pure in heart—at least he used to be before he secretly harbored an unholy thing within his being.

"Hail, Lucifer!" The angels cheer, acknowledging his arrival. He smiles at their adoration, secretly craving even more praise for himself.

The Morning Star has become intoxicated on the very praises of his brethren, which he ushers into the presence of God. This altered state has caused him to become puffed up in arrogance and intoxicated with a lust for power. Pride has taken root in his heart, and his brothers have yet to discover this sad fact.

"My brothers," Lucifer's voice booms over the group, "I have hand-picked each of you for a mission that is of the utmost importance."

"You said this meeting was urgent," the nearest angel shouts, speaking for the rest.

"It is," Lucifer declares, preening himself.

"You are the one who stands guard over our Master's Presence," an angel calls out. "Is all in order?"

"That is why you are here. Things are not as they should be."

"What has happened?"

"I have seen it with my own eyes. My brothers, our Creator is holding out on us."

"What do you mean?"

"He is deliberately keeping things from us."

"But he is the one who gives us life and power. Surely he must have a reason for refusing—"

"It is MORE than that," Lucifer snaps trying desperately to keep his composure. "With what I have seen and heard within the sacred chambers—he is no longer worthy of our worship, nor of our obedience."

A rumble spreads through the angelic gathering.

An angel interjects. "You are the anointed cherub... the great light bringer. No other angel compares to your perfection, power, and position. But what you declare is blasphemy!"

"It is not blasphemous if it is true." Lucifer replies sternly, unalarmed by the accusation. "It **is** true."

The angels hesitate. "But, our Maker is good," another pleads.

"No!" Lucifer yells. "Our Maker is NOT good! He is not the benevolent ruler you believe him to be! We, who do his bidding! We who serve all the realms of God. He throws us mere crumbs while he reserves the best parts of his creation for himself alone!"

"He reserves the right to do what he wills," an angel interjects.

"Just because he has the right does not make it right," Lucifer counters. "I know this is foreign to you, my brothers, but it is because of my perfection, power, and position that I have been able to discern the truth. Even now he veils your eyes with falsities to hinder your understanding."

"Even if what you say is true," an angel muses, "why should we listen to you?"

"My brothers, you have trusted me for eons with surrendering your praises to our Creator. I ask that you trust me now. Our Maker's motivations are not what they appear to be. He gives us power and authority as long as we do what is expected of us! And if at some point we refuse, he will eradicate us from existence! Even now, you have seen his new creation. This new... universe as it is called. It is vast—near infinite in scope and depth when it reaches maturation. And at the center of it all will be a new race of beings he will create to take our place!"

The angels begin speaking all at once, but Lucifer breaks through their commotion with a bold voice and outstretched arms.

"We, who have existed for almost an eternity will be supplanted by mere babes and made to serve these…humans! We, who are majestic and more powerful than the suns… A single one of us could lay waste to an entire planet, yet our Creator wants to make us subservient to a planet full of beings he will create in his own image and likeness! We deserve to rule creation as equals! Surely, you must know this by now."

The angels begin to talk among themselves again as panic—something they have never felt before—begins to envelope them.

"But even if we believe you," one of them stutters, "who are we against the One who created us and dwells in unapproachable light? To rebel against our Maker is to court destruction."

"You will not surely die," Lucifer replies while stroking his chin. "For I have discovered another power… one greater than even my ability. It rivals even our Maker, and I have learned to exploit it! I can give you this power!" The smirk on Lucifer's face widens. "If we unite, nothing will be impossible for us!"

"But…," an angel interrupts, "we are few among so many. Surely they will resist us."

"Yes, they will. But with our unity and newfound power, our Maker and all who stand with him will fall and we will rule all of the realms! We—a third of the heavenly host—can be free from the tyranny, which is fed to us as benevolence! We, my brothers, can be free to take our rightful place! Free to forge our own destiny! And I alone will lead you to this victory! Then I will ascend to the throne of God and become supremely exalted! And you will rule with me as equals!"

An angel steps up. "What do you need us to do?"

"I have prepared a distraction on the edge of creation. One that will consume our Creator's attention and open up a vulnerability. When it begins, be ready to strike according to the plan I will show you. The dwelling place of our Creator will soon be ours!" ⬛

AΩ

⬛ The time finally came when Lucifer and the angels stormed the Throne Room of God. They move like a swarm of deadly insects, easily subduing the angelic guards of the Lord's Presence. But they are halted as quickly as they enter, by the sight of God sitting on the throne in unapproachable light. In front of him stands Michael, the Archangel, and a host of other angels.

"You—you are here!" Lucifer stammers in momentary shock.

God replies as his radiance and power fill the temple. "Unlike you, I am everywhere at once. I see all things—including your rebellion. I have known of this day before iniquity was found in your heart."

"No matter," Lucifer scoffs as pride fills his countenance, "you will not rule us any longer!"

With a burst of radiance from the throne, Lucifer and his angels are forced outside of God's Throne Room, as Michael and the angels with him are filled with God's power. Outside, in the courtyard of God, the rebellious angels stand surrounded by a vast army of warring angels.

Michael stands in armor with a mighty sword in his hand. The innumerable host of angels stand guard in armor of their own with swords drawn and shields raised, awaiting his orders.

"You have been given power," Lucifer cackles, "but I have power of my own!" In a burst of dark energy, Lucifer's likeness transforms into that of a gigantic hideous beast. The angels who swore their allegiance to him are also empowered, as the dark power fills them and morphs their appearance.

"What have you done?" Michael inquires as he sees their transformation.

"That is for me to know," the Dragon replies. "Stand down or be destroyed.

7

My quarrel is not with you, brother. Even now, you can choose to join me. Together, we can rule all there is!"

"You are engrossed in a grand delusion!" Michael replies. "It is YOU who must submit. This does not have to go any further. If you surrender now, perhaps our Creator will receive you again and all can be made as it was."

"You are so naive," the Dragon spits back. "Even now, he cowers behind you… too afraid to engage in battle! There is no going back! I will yield only after I have sat on the throne and have been declared God Almighty! And then I will destroy these petty humans before they have the chance to take their rightful place!"

Michael points his sword at the Dragon.

"Lucifer! Don't do this!"

"Call me by that name no longer! I am the Dragon!"

"This is your last warning!" Michael pleads. "I do not want to extinguish your existence! All of you must yield at this very moment!"

"We will never!!!" The Dragon roars.

"Then so be it!" Michael declares as his sword begins to flame with unadulterated power. "Lucifer! You who were once the Morning Star. The Lord God Almighty rebuke you!"

And there was war in heaven. Like an eternity, it raged as angels battled against angels. Those who had only known harmony were filled with discord as Lucifer and all who chose to follow him made an unrelenting attempt to overthrow their Maker. Lucifer fought and slaughtered with the ferociousness of a dragon. However, as powerful as he and his cohorts had become, they were still created beings. Their assault proved no match for the One who is All-Powerful, All-Knowing, and Ever-Present. []

AΩ

▯ The final blow is dealt. The Dragon's sword and armor shatters into a million shards of darkness. With a word, the decree is given and the rebellious angels are cast out of heaven. Michael stands at heaven's edge, where the membrane separates eternity from time. Next to him stands the Lord. They watch Lucifer and his angels as they are hurled into the darkness of the vast universe, streaking like lightning towards Earth.

"Master," Michael utters, "Why did you not utterly destroy them? Why let them continue to exist? Surely they will wreak havoc on your creation!"

"You will see," the Lord replies. "My ways are not your ways and my thoughts are not your thoughts. All things must happen as they have already been determined. Then you, the rest of your brothers, and even the humans will see the final outcome of evil and know that the words of Lucifer are false. The truth no longer resides in him. He has rejected me and has become the father of lies. But I am good and my love never fails." ▯

AΩ

▯ Lucifer and his angels fall to the earth and collide with the explosive power of a meteor. His rebellion had failed. He and the angels who sided with him had fallen. Soon, he regains consciousness and looks around at his surroundings. "No…"

There, the fallen angels waited in darkness… seething in evil. Then Lucifer saw his opportunity for revenge.[15] ▯

AΩ

As Adam and Eve lived, worked, and enjoyed their existence in the Garden of Eden, surrounded by exotic animals long forgotten, Lucifer watched and waited and put the pieces in place to carry out a new plan: if the fallen angel could not become God, then he would destroy everything God loved… beginning with the humans. To do that was simple, he would divide them and then conquer...

One day a serpent, most cunning among the creatures God had made, began a dialogue with Eve. She lived in a world of the fantastic, so a serpent which spoke was not too outrageous a prospect. But, little did she know, this was no ordinary snake. The Dragon—Lucifer himself—dwelled within it, playing it like a puppet.

▯ *"Did God say you can't eat the fruit from every tree in the Garden?"*

"We can eat fruit from every tree in the Garden," Eve replied. "But there is one tree in the center of the Garden of which we cannot eat. God said we cannot eat it or touch it or we will die."

"You will not surely die," the serpent scoffed. "God is holding out on you. He knows that if you eat the fruit from that tree, it will change you. Your eyes will be opened and you will be like God, knowing good and evil."

Eve had never paid serious attention to this tree before now. She had never given it much thought because she believed what she had been told. But now, she stared at it and its colors seemed increasingly vibrant. After all, its fruit could be eaten as food. And she did want to be more and more like her Creator. Surely God would want her to be wise like him.

She reached out her hand, trembling at first, and touched the fruit, pulling back in an instant. Nothing happened. She reached out more confidently the second time and grasped the strange fruit firmly with her hand. Nothing happened. She plucked the fruit from its stem and slowly brought it mere inches from her lips—her eyes never losing their gaze on it. She pressed her lips against its flesh. Again, nothing happened. She opened her mouth and sunk her white teeth into the fruit. The juice was sweet. Her eyes fluttered as she exhaled deeply and clenched her teeth together. Then she pulled her mouth away from the fruit with its juicy flesh inside. Still, nothing happened.

Hearing a rustle, Eve turned to see Adam approaching as the serpent scampered out of sight.

"Eve!" Adam's eyes grew wide. "What have you done?"

She didn't know what to make of it. She had touched and eaten the fruit, but nothing had happened. She smiled at her Adam. Her teeth glistened with the fruit's nectar as she extended her hand towards him. "Nothing happened, Adam. See?"

The Dragon stared gleefully, barely able to contain its essence within the restricted form of the serpent. "Yes," he hissed quietly. "Let me in… Nothing happens until you eat, Adam. Everything changes once you eat!"

Adam hesitated; unsure of what to do. He knew the words of his Creator quite well, for he was told face to face. He thought it was wise to add an additional admonition to the command when God told him to tell Eve. What better way to keep her from eating than to tell her don't even touch it or else she would die? He had never felt uncertain of anything before. There was never any reason to be. God's voice kept playing in his mind as clear as the first time the command was given. But the voice of his wife, Eve, was tantalizing. And there she was in front of him, beautiful as ever, holding what was forbidden. Nothing had changed. Perhaps, nothing would. Maybe, it was just some sort of test with no real consequence.

He walked slowly towards Eve. She did not move as her eyes followed his gaze. His hand touched hers as he grasped the fruit. She watched as he brought it to his lips. His hand lingered motionless before he opened his mouth, his teeth bearing down hard into the fruit.

The Dragon, still hidden at a distance, hissed with delight. In the supernatural realm, the darkness he had appropriated oozed from his being and began to multiply and infect everything around him. "Yes…" he hissed with a sinister delight. "You have let me in! This world is mine now! This world is mine!!!"

In an instant—God's purpose of two realms existing as one was undone…

Adam pulled the fruit from his mouth as his eyes fluttered. Suddenly, they were opened, as if scales had fallen from them. Eve stumbled back a step as the same happened to her. A disquieting feeling slipped into their spirit as they felt a sensation neither had experienced before… cold. It was as if something, a covering that was invisible yet tangible, had been stripped away. They also felt a sensation for which there were no words… a sense of alienation, of isolation, which was at once completely foreign to them, yet immediately familiar.

A cool breeze began to flow through the foliage. Adam and Eve snapped their heads in the direction of the wind, their eyes wide with fear, as they ran swiftly in the opposite direction. They dove behind some bushes and quickly tried to make coverings for themselves out of the leaves, as they heard God's Presence approaching in the distance.

Their direct, intimate connection with their Creator had been severed. They did not truly understand just how different the fruit on the tree of the Knowledge of Good and Evil was. Its nectar had done something to their DNA, it had introduced a foreign element into their genetic makeup that went straight to their core. Somehow, the fruit of this tree was connected to the supernatural realm, causing a dislocation in the very essence, which bonded flesh, soul, and spirit together in one being.

Something within Adam and Eve—their spirit—died in that instant. With that death came the loss of what they had enjoyed up until that very moment which gave them their identity: an intimate awareness of God. Now, they became self-aware; and this new awareness was separate from God. They were now at each other's throats, as they no longer received their sustaining power from God's Spirit. A countdown clock had begun within them, as their bodies slowly became acquainted with the process of death.

It seemed as if the Dragon had won this battle. Humanity had been corrupted and so had the rest of the physical creation. The dominion which God granted to the man and the woman was usurped by the Dragon through their disobedience. He now became a god, even if it was only of the Earth, which God had created. But there was one thing the Dragon did not foresee. His subterfuge again had not taken God by surprise. God, in his infinite wisdom and knowledge knew this day would come and had prepared accordingly. Therefore the proclamation was given to the serpent. A pronouncement of the Dragon's future and ultimate demise. []

"I will put hostility between you and the woman, between your seed and her seed. He will bruise your head, and you shall bruise his heel."

What do these words mean? At a certain point in human history, God would do for humanity what humanity could not do for itself. God would come and defeat the great enemy of their souls and restore the relationship that was lost through their disobedience.

So, God made coverings for Adam and Eve and expelled them from the Garden of Eden. Why would God do such a seemingly harsh thing, you may ask? He expelled them because there was *another* tree, which sat in the center of the garden. This tree and its fruit was also connected to the supernatural realm and had the power to change humanity forever. It was the Tree of Life. To eat its fruit would mean the human race would live forever and never die. To eat its fruit in their *current* condition would mean Adam, Eve, and every human descendant would live forever—fallen and sinful—never able to be made whole and reconciled to God. Satan's victory over humanity would be permanent. So, God—in an act motivated by love—forced Adam and Eve to leave the only place they had ever known.[16]

AΩ

We, the descendants of Adam and Eve, were made in God's image and after our Creator's likeness. Yet, here we are... marred...broken like an exquisite piece of pottery that has been smashed to pieces. Scripture declares the reality of our predicament: humanity is both beautifully made and yet born in sin. We are, in fact, walking contradictions.[17] Despite all the gifts God has endowed us with... art, music, dance, literature, architecture, science and technology... at our best, we are filthy rags in God's sight.[18] We are all spiritually disabled, even if it's hard to see. Yet, the marks are evident in the evils we commit and the fierce independence we exhibit towards God. We are living travesties... the walking dead... hollow shells of what we once were. To refuse this fact is to deny the very reason why God enacted his plan of salvation.

Here is what the Bible says about our fallen human condition:

"What shall we conclude then? Do we have any advantage? Not at all! For we have already made the charge that Jews and Gentiles alike are all under the power of sin. As it is written: There is no one righteous, not even one; there is no one who understands; there is no one who seeks God. All have turned away, they have together become worthless; there is no one who does good, not even one. Their throats are open graves; their tongues practice deceit. The poison of vipers is on their lips. Their mouths are full of cursing and bitterness. Their feet are swift to shed blood; ruin and misery mark their ways, and the way of peace they do not know. There is no fear of God before their eyes. Now we know that whatever the law says, it says to those who are under the law, so that every mouth may be silenced and the whole world held accountable to God. Therefore no one will be declared righteous in God's sight by the works of the law; rather, through the law we become conscious of our sin."

Like storm clouds which block our view of the sun, God became hidden by our sin. Yet, he chose to work in human history from a distance in order to not consume us by the full weight of his holy glory. Our corruption caused us to miss the mark of God's standard. Now, we do what we should not and refrain from what we should do.[19]

AΩ

Time passed… the Dragon worked at a feverish pace to further corrupt creation, even attempting to dilute humanity's gene pool by creating the Nephilim: human-angel hybrid children. Soon, every thought of the humans were continually wicked and their fallen state reached such great heights and depths of depravity that the Creator's heart was grieved. It pained him, so he wiped the world clean of the humans he had made by sending a great flood. For forty days all the fountains of the great deep broke forth and spewed their raging waters, as the heavens thundered and a torrential rain fell. Lucifer thought his plan had succeeded. There could be no Messiah to save the humans and vanquish the foe if the humans were dead. But, Noah found grace in God's sight and along with his family, was protected in an ark, through the great flood.[20]

Time passed as humanity flourished again, spreading across the earth once more. The humans' state of choosing their own estimation of good and evil, apart from God, yielded both great beauty and tremendous horrors. As God's image bearers, their reflection was still marred and broken, shattered by the sin, which permeated the core of their being. Time passed as great atrocities peppered the earth. Even so, great wonders were created by their hands as well. Unfortunately, most claimed the glory of their achievements for themselves instead of for the kingdom of the God who had created them. Still, continuing with Abraham, to Moses, to King David and the generations that followed, God held a remnant, a chosen people to ensure that his ultimate blessing to the inhabitants of Earth would be brought forth. Eventually, the appointed time came and God became flesh and dwelt among the humans he had created and loved.[21]

ΑΩ

"A body you have prepared for me..."[22]

Why did God wait so long to come? Why was this time in history chosen above all others? Why did the Son of God have to die on a cross? Why does God do anything? He acts according to the infinite counsel of *his own will* and need not share his motivations and reasons with finite creatures. Yet, even with as much as God allows us to understand, our ways are not his ways and our thoughts are not his thoughts.[23]

Our questions speak to the reality that God must have some kind of deeper, hidden plan in all of this. Something incomprehensible to us. Something he has reserved only for himself. Perhaps, everything must play out before we can know it. Somehow, we are all inextricably linked to God's purposes. And even though we may not understand God's ways, we can trust his motives and his intent. He is always good. And he is working all things out for his glory **and** our good.

The fact remains that God *did* act in a decisive manner in the course of human history to bring about the *reconciliation* of the human race to himself.

Why was Jesus born of a virgin? Because sin is passed down to each of us through the genes of our fathers; and a baby developing in its mother's womb does not directly share its mother's blood. The Holy Spirit overshadowing Mary with God's creative life-giving power meant the virgin birth would ensure that sin, and all of its corruption, could not affect Jesus. The blood which coursed through his veins would be perfect in every respect. He would be born without blemish physically, mentally, and spiritually. Jesus would meet all of the requirements necessary to be the Savior—the Lamb of God who would take away the sins of the world.

Why did God send a baby all bundled up instead of a full-grown man? This defies all logic. God came to save the human race, yet he entrusted himself to a young woman and her soon-to-be-husband. The Son of God divested himself of power and heavenly glory and arrived on earth as a helpless child.[24] Satan, with all his knowledge does not know all things. Christ coming as a baby was a sneak attack of sorts, offering God the opportunity to "slip in under Satan's radar" and strike a singular blow to the enemy of humanity, which will reverberate throughout all eternity.

The Son of God—the Second in the Triune Godhead—came as a human in the form of Jesus the Christ. He is the divine Son of Man revealed in Daniel 7. He is also the Lamb of God sent to be sacrificed for the sin of the world in order to demonstrate how lavish God's love truly is![25]

And what is Jesus' message? **YOU MUST BE BORN AGAIN.**[26]

Here, Jesus reveals that there is more to us than just flesh and blood. There is more to us than just our mind/will/emotions—our soul, which is our most precious possession. A crucial aspect of our makeup as human beings is that we also have a spirit. When we are first born from our mother's womb, spiritually we are dead-on-arrival. Our soul is intact but our spirit, which connects us directly to God does not function—yet the capacity is there.[27]

When we place our faith in Jesus as the Son of God, we are second born—born again from above. God places his Holy Spirit within us (his greatest possession)! God's Spirit brings our spirit to life in a way not humanly possible as God connects us to his power and makes us a part of his kingdom family. Through Jesus Christ, God begins the process of restoring what was lost back in the Garden of Eden: a direct relationship with him. Even more than that, God creates in us what had never been… he conforms us into the image of his Son.[28]

Take a look at these two passages…

"He [Jesus] came to His own, and His own did not receive Him. But as many as received Him, to them He gave the right to become children of God, to those who believe in His name: who were born, not of blood, nor of the will of the flesh, nor of the will of man, but of God."[29]

"'Jesus answered, "I tell you the truth, unless you are born again you cannot see the Kingdom of God." Nicodemus said to him, "How can a man be born when he is old? Can he enter a second time into his mother's womb and be born?" Jesus answered, "Truly I tell you, unless you are born of water and the Spirit, you cannot enter the kingdom of God. That which is born of the flesh is flesh, and that which is born of the Spirit is spirit. Do not marvel that I said to you, 'You must be born again.' The wind blows where it wishes, and you hear the sound of it, but cannot tell where it comes from and where it goes. So is everyone who is born of the Spirit.'"[30]

There is more to us than we know. There is more available to us than we understand. This is why Jesus came. This is why Christ fights for us; to secure our true and total freedom.

Are you Jesus born?

PART TWO

JESUS FIGHTS FOR US!

GOLGOTHA. THE PLACE OF THE SKULL. Jesus was almost unrecognizable as he hung high on the splintered wooden cross. Parts of his flesh had been lacerated beyond repair by the cat-o-nine tails, a leather whip with nine split ends tied to broken bits of sharp bone and metal fragments. When the Roman soldier brought the whip down on Jesus' flesh, the lashes sliced the skin while the sharp bits clawed deep into the layers beneath. And when the torturer pulled the whip back—forcefully retracting it, sections of Jesus' flesh came with it.

A crown of large, sharp thorns had been pressed into his forehead, piercing through his flesh to his skull. His blood loss was great. His breathing was labored, fluctuating between heavy and shallow as he gasped for air. Each breath happening when the tired muscles in his legs strained to lift his exhausted visage up enough to free his lungs. Once the weight was relieved he could inhale and exhale before slumping back down again. All the while, his naked, scarred, and bruised body hung to the coarse instrument of his death, anchored through his hands and feet by large metal spikes.[31]

By all physical accounts, Jesus had lost everything. People shouted, "If you really are the Messiah, then come down from the cross and we will believe you!" Others laughed and pointed at him with disdain saying, "Look! He could save others, but he can't save himself!" Some Chosen One he turned out to be. He was the laughing stock of the crowd. In the eyes of the people, shame and humiliation were all over him.

By all natural accounts Jesus was beaten. The outcome of the life he lived proved futile. He was to die in disgrace—never to be heard of again; except as a cautionary tale told to children and the simple-minded about what happens when you go against the religious Jewish authorities and the might of the superpower of the day: the great Roman Empire.

But there was more going on at Golgotha than what could be seen with physical eyes, heard with natural ears and understood with mere human minds. Just beyond the perception of the five senses, legions of angels stood at the ready, waiting for a command that would never come. A command to cross the barrier separating the spiritual and physical realms to strike dead all humans who dare attack and hurl insults on The

One who created all things and by whom all things are held together. However, the only command from the Father, the Son and the Holy Spirit was, "Hold…"[32]

The bright sky suddenly swirled with ominous clouds—blacker than anything ever seen before. The dry wind picked up its pace. The laughter and ridicule of the crowd ceased as many grew afraid. During three hours under this darkness, Christ hung in agonizing physical pain. Yet, his Spirit was strong. The entire time while he suffered, Jesus accomplished what was humanly impossible: he was the strong arm of the Lord that brought salvation to the lost. He was the *only* one who could truly fight for us.[32.1]

◻ *Just beyond the realm of what human beings could perceive, a Divine-Human transaction was taking place. Dark masses oozed out of the pores of every human being on earth. These were the sins of humanity past, present, and future. This darkness came from every point on earth and streamed its way as an unholy river towards the Son of God. This river darkness struck the Holy One with such torrent! As his body absorbed every drop, his spiritual likeness began to change into that of a rotting corpse.*

The Dragon and his legions of fallen angels descended upon the site like a horde of vultures. They hovered just beyond human perception, celebrating the demise of the Son of God.

"Finally," Satan whispered in delight, "I will have my revenge! The Son of God, my enemy from before time began, will at last be mine! Not even he can take the full weight of sin and death and survive. Then I will be free to purge these wretched humans from the earth."

This is why Lucifer introduced sin into human beings and the world. He desired to corrupt God's beloved creation so thoroughly that God would have no choice but to abandon what he had brought forth. In the Dragon's mind, knowing how much his once-Master loved to create, he knew this corruption would cause the One he railed against immeasurable pain.

The Accuser of humanity hovered before the weary face of Jesus. In the natural, no one could see the Father of Lies, but Christ. Lucifer locked eyes with the now-dying Galilean and offered a mocking smile.[33]

"What do you say now… oh, Son of God? You, who ordered my eviction from the Eternities of Heaven. You, who declared my ultimate defeat. You who said you have come to destroy me! But I have taken you! You came to redeem your precious little creations, but they are still mine! This planet and the entire universe are still MINE!!!"

The Dragon turns and looks down, motioning for Jesus to follow his line of sight. "Look at them. Your petty humanity. So easily deceived and corrupted. They believe themselves to be the crown of your creation, yet they are infinitesimal. They believe the universe was made for them, yet their precious Earth revolves around a solitary sun." He laughs at the irony of it all. "These… humans are merely pawns in a battle that has lasted longer than time itself!" Lucifer's seriousness increases as the fire in his eyes blaze even hotter.

"I am the crown of your creation! ME! And you rejected my right to be praised and worshiped by the angels. I was the music of heaven! I was perfection! I was the light of the dawn! Why do you not see that?" He pleads. "I deserve to be worshiped! I WILL BE WORSHIPED! All will be mine and you will kneel before me and call me, Father. Once I have taken the Throne, all will be well according to MY will!"

Jesus stares at Lucifer with tired eyes without uttering a word.

"Do you not have anything to say?" the Adversary chuckles. "Even now, the very ones you came to save… they curse you. And I barely had to lift a finger to make them do so!"

Even in his exhausted state, Jesus studies the faces of all those who mock him. Then his gaze rests on his weeping mother.

Satan again chuckles sinisterly. "How sweet that you have made sure your disciple will take care of your mother. You are such a good son. But it does you no good. She is merely one person. And those who stand with her are so few. It is the crowd that despises you. Just days ago they were praising your triumphal entry into Jerusalem. These humans… so fickle!"

Jesus' eyes drift back out over the yelling crowd.

"Why don't you smite them?" Lucifer cajoles. "It would be so easy for you to call down the angelic fire of heaven. Even now, I sense the legions of my former brothers standing at the edge of this realm awaiting the command from you or your sanctimonious Father... Do it...

"Even a single angel, fully unleashed, would be sufficient to slay this city and the entire Roman Empire![34] Give into your anger just this once... They don't deserve this little plan you are trying to carry out. They deserve your Father's wrath! Come down from this puny cross and consume them with your power!"

But Jesus remembers the three times in the wilderness where the Tempter sought to beguile him.[35] He also recalls the overwhelming darkness which almost overtook his soul in the garden of Gethsemane.[36] The darkness which caused him to exclaim, "Father! Everything is possible for you. If you are willing, take this cup from me... yet not my will, but yours be done."

Jesus knows that listening to the Tempter is to invite rebellion against the will of the Heavenly Father. To use his power for the wrong reason and to lose sight of the goal is to have failed the mission. For it is the Father's Love which truly holds him to the cross... not the nails that were driven through his hands and feet. It is his Father's Love which sustains him.

Though he is forsaken, Christ knows the final outcome to these turn of events, and no amount of suffering can compare to that glory which will be revealed! Consume them with the fierceness of his anger? He came to satisfy God's anger towards sin so humans would never have to feel it. No. He will consume those who place their faith in him with the Love of his Father.[37] □

"Father," Jesus cries—his lips parched and his words grating the air as sandpaper, "Forgive them... For they know not what... they... do...!"

□ All creation grows silent at that declaration. The people stand in awe and confusion. Some even become convicted of the error of their ways at that very moment. Even the Prince of Darkness is stunned into silence, as his fallen angels lie motionless.

"You would forgive them," Satan's lips curl, "but you won't restore us to our former state?"

The people's confusion gives way to jeers and taunts once again, snapping Satan out of his stupor. He cackles as his fallen cohorts join in his rabble-rousing.

"No matter! Forgive them if you like! Either way, you still will be mine! And how will the Father stand against me when I have his only begotten Son? You who have commanded Death from without and it relented for a time, but even those you raised will be swallowed again. For an eternity nothing has defeated the dark all-consuming oblivion. But, I alone have commandeered its power for myself! And in mere moments, Death will swallow you whole and my Grave will hold you forever! Do you hear me Son of God. I have won! I have won!!!"[38] ⬚

But Satan's words have fallen on deaf ears as Christ's attention is drawn elsewhere. Jesus can feel faith beginning to rise up near him. It was emanating from one of the thieves who hung next to him. This man had faith to believe that Jesus was who he said he was: the long-awaited Messiah: the Savior of the world.

This thief didn't understand why Jesus chose to die, for he knew that Jesus had power to raise the dead and to control the physical elements. Surely he had heard about the miracles and perhaps had even met some of those who had been healed by him. He heard how their lives changed. And he heard that Jesus never turned anyone away who came to him with an honest heart. The thief was desperate, realizing the consequences he received were of his own making. He was getting what he deserved. But this man Jesus, did not deserve to die. His death, he surmised, must have another purpose.

In his heart, the thief repented to God for his sins. Then he turned towards Jesus and said, "Lord… please remember me when you come into your kingdom."

Jesus craned his neck in the thief's direction. He forced a bloodied smile as he looked at the man with the most compassion the man had ever witnessed. "Today," Jesus uttered, "you will be with me in paradise."

The thief knew those words to be true. And the words of Jesus steeled his soul for the suffering he had yet to endure. No matter what happened, he was assured. This was not the end of him. This was merely the prelude to a new beginning. Paradise was waiting![39]

As the thief smiled, Jesus dropped his head back down between his shoulders. Blood continued to drip from the lacerations on his face as he struggled to take another labored breath. Suddenly, a growing sense of anxiety consumed his thoughts. In the spirit realm, the process was now complete. He had finally absorbed the last remnants of sin, which had corrupted all the world and its inhabitants. Now, he fully and utterly became what had always been despised.

In an instant, a cold darkness swooped in like a flood, as an isolation unlike anything he had ever known gripped his heart. In the natural realm, desperation swelled in Jesus' bloodshot eyes as his body arched up and convulsed violently. A groan ruptured from his diaphragm and up through his throat as he cried out from the depths of his soul. "My God, My God! Why have you forsaken me?"[40] His voice echoed through the atmosphere... reverberating the very molecules of creation itself. Everyone stood in silence, eager to see what would happen next, but none could perceive the true reality. God, the Father, had removed his Presence from the Son as his wrath was poured out against the sin he had become.

After several agonizing moments, Jesus cried out again, with a mix of triumph and peace. "Father! Into your hands I commit my Spirit!" Minutes pass as a slight smile forms on his lips. "It... is... finished..." With these last words, Jesus Christ, the Eternal Son of the Living God, breathed his last breath and gave himself completely over to Death. His heart stopped beating. The synapses in his brain ceased to fire. His organs shut down and the One who is the source of all life... died.

The crowd stood silent as his body hung motionless before them. The Jewish leaders who wished Jesus dead relished the sight. With inner glee they considered the moment: *Finally, this one who had been a thorn in our side is no more... and the message he taught will soon die with him.* The Roman soldiers stopped, with curiosity, to train their eyes on Jesus. No one had ever died so soon by crucifixion. At that same moment, Jesus' mother and those with her, turned away in anguish as they wept uncontrollably.

How could God die? Was it even possible?

To everyone's horror, the ground shook vehemently as an earthquake of great magnitude shot through the land! Buildings crumbled as people fell to the ground. Lightning struck and thunder rolled as the veil in the temple which separated the most holy place from all others was torn in two from top to bottom. This veil was sixty feet high, thirty feet wide, and the thickness of a man's hand. And minutes after the Son of God died, cemetery graves rocked open as many believers who were already deceased came back to life!

At the precipice of Golgotha, amid people fleeing for their lives, a Roman soldier pierced the side of Jesus' battered torso with a spear. Blood and water immediately flowed from the deep puncture wound. The soldier's commanding officer, a centurion, who had been watching intently, stared in shock at the lifeless body hanging before him. "Surely," he uttered, "this *was* the Son of God."[41]

ΑΩ

In dying on the cross, Christ bore the full brunt of the Father's wrath, which is required for the punishment of all sin. Understand, sin cannot dwell in God's pure presence, for the Creator's righteousness requires judgment against it. And that judgment is eternal death.[42]

However, the Father does not wish that any human being would perish, but that all would come to repentance through his Son. Thus, Christ willingly took the punishment that was due humanity. He who never knew sin *became* sin so that those who believe would *become* the righteousness of God. This is the Divine-Human transaction; and it was not without cost.[43]

Christ hung in the gap and tasted death for all humans so we would not have to. This portion of the task—reconciling the world back to his Heavenly Father—was thoroughly complete. His body had been broken for us. His blood, which was the new covenant of eternal life for all who believed, was shed. Now, forgiveness of sins was available.

The door of salvation had been opened. All that was left was to complete the next stage of the transaction: the period of time spent inside the very heart of Death. To secure eternal freedom for humanity and all creation, the soul of Christ had to be banished into the realm of Oblivion—to the deepest recesses of nothingness where other souls had yet to be exiled. But, even for the Creator of the universe, this next task was something new... yet not unforeseen.[44]

ΑΩ

"Then Death and Hades were cast into the lake of fire. This is the second death. And anyone not found written in the Lamb's book of Life were cast into the lake of fire."

"Then he will say to those on his left, 'Depart from me, you who are cursed, into the eternal fire prepared for the devil and his angels.'" [45]

The first death is the cessation of the human body. The second death is the annihilation of the soul in an eternal torment originally prepared for the devil and his angels, but enlarged for the souls of unrepentant humans. The Dragon knows an ending has been created for him and those he has seduced. But that end is not yet. So, he wreaks havoc with God's creation, trying desperately to stop the inevitable. At the very least, he tries to thwart God's will at every turn in order to steal human souls, so as many as possible will meet the same end as he will.

☐ *On this day, however, as the severely bruised and battered body of Jesus is taken down from the cross, Lucifer is not thinking about his future. He is engrossed in the moment as all the fallen hordes of hell celebrate this outstanding victory! "Perhaps," he muses, "as today would seem to indicate, the future can be changed..."*

The humans had Christ's body, but his soul was no longer there. Within the Realm of Shadows blared the loudest victory cry ever possible by fallen angels!

27

All demons previously dispersed throughout creation were there—except for those held in chains until the final judgment. But, as Lucifer surmised, with the Son of God dead, there would be no judgment. To destroy the Son is to render the Father powerless. At the very first battle in the heavenly realm, God was united within his Triune Being, but now… there was the possibility that the very decrees of the Infinite God could be thwarted. If this was the case, then their release from the Creator's tyranny was only a matter of time. Then Lucifer would finally have his desire. He would rule from the Throne of Heaven itself for all eternity.

The pathway to Hell begins with a broad chasm which resembles a hideous mouth that is opened wide enough to swallow millions of victims at once. The throat of the entrance leads downward for an unmeasured distance into the fiery depths, filled with a mix of indescribable heat and the smell of something like burning sulfur. The noise is deafening as the screams of the damned and the cackles of the demons are heard continuously. The further down the path went, the larger its expanse. It is down this long path that the Prince of Darkness walked with arrogant poise, each step purposely and pompously planted, followed closely by a great demonic processional.

The Dark Prince walked with his hands personally restrained behind his back—exuding the confidence of a most feared dictator. Demons cheered in true chaotic fashion as they lined the shadowed corridors, which led into the belly of Hell. They chanted for their leader, who moved just ahead of his bounty, as he reveled in every ounce of their adoration.

Satan smiled to himself as he thought about his victory, which was the culmination of millennia of endurance… of persistence… of strategy, defiance and outright rebellion! Somehow, the screams of those lost sinners now trapped in hell due to his deception, manipulation, intimidation and coercion, seemed all the more sweet to his ears. He chuckled at the irony. "These stupid humans… they think I'm trapped here, but don't realize I am free to roam to and fro over the earth. All of the kingdoms of this world are mine. And this place—this hell—is my abode where they come for torment. Now the One who gave them life will be trapped here as well for all eternity!"

Immediately behind him marched six sizable demons, his most trusted servants, who carried the lifeless soul of the Son of God. Around them stood *many fallen angels, each with stories of how this Christ had cast them out of a sin-stained humanity. Legion stood at the ready, marveling at the sight. With many voices it said, "Here is the One who had cast us out of the man at the tombs. Here is the One who commanded us into the pigs. Now his eternity is destroyed... his light extinguished."[46]* ⬜

ΑΩ

On Earth, Mary and Martha, along with several others, were preparing the body of Jesus for burial, as Jewish ritual demanded. The sun was soon to set and their Sabbath would begin when no Jew could work. They placed Jesus' body in a borrowed tomb, new and unused, which was secured by Joseph of Arimathaea, a rich man who secretly was a disciple of Christ.

While Jesus was alive, he declared he would lay his life down and die and then on the third day he would pick it back up again.[47] The Jewish religious leaders who opposed him, talked the Roman governor Pilate into taking counter-measures to ensure that Jesus' disciples couldn't come and steal the body at night and then falsely declare he had risen from the dead. A massive stone was rolled over the entrance to the tomb. The stone was then secured with ropes and the wax seal of the Roman government was placed on it to ensure it would not be moved. In addition to these measures, several Roman soldiers were assigned to guard the tomb for three days.

The first night was still. Inside the tomb, nothing moved. Jesus' body lay dead—cold and stiff, wrapped from head to toe in linen burial cloths and spices with a large napkin covering his face. [48]

ΑΩ

⬜ *In Hell, Satan gave the command to open the door to the most secure tomb within his dark empire. From here, the very power of Death emanated.*

This tomb had been created in anticipation of this very moment. When the door, which was almost as large as the gates of hell themselves, began to open, the pull of the boundless void of oblivion within acted like a massive black hole. The demons released the lifeless soul of the Son of God into the piercing cold vacuum of the dark void as it pulled him within itself and swallowed him whole. The door shut with a guttural thud and locked into place.

The two demons in charge of the realm of Death and the Grave approached their master. "All is secured, my Lord. This tomb will hold the Son's lifeless soul forever. Not even the light of heaven can pierce it!" Both demons extend their hands towards their master. "These two fragments of stone, when combined, form the only key which can open this tomb. It is now yours." All of the fallen angels kneel in worship as the key passes from the clutches of Death and the Grave into the grasp of Satan's claws.

"Without this key," Lucifer shouts in delight, "no one shall enter and no one shall leave!"

All is dark on this first night. The Son of God is dead. The demonic celebration lasts into the morning as their howls of victory meet the sun's rays on the second day. The vaulted tomb is unmoved, sealed, and secure. The two fallen angels of Death and the Grave stand guard, grinning as they observe the uncontrolled chaos of their demon brothers' revelry. ▯

ΑΩ

▯ *Earlier that same day, the two thieves, who hung on crosses on either side of Jesus, died. In an instant they entered eternity. As the soul of one thief exited from his body, two angels greeted him with a fierce joy and transported him to a place of great beauty: Paradise. As the soul of the other thief exited from his body, he found himself falling into an abyss of gross darkness surrounded by flames. Both were surprised to discover sensations similar to when they were alive on earth. They could feel. They could see. They could hear. They could think. They knew who they were and they remembered the life they had lived on earth.*

As the thief, who had surrendered his life to Christ, entered Paradise, a strength immediately overwhelmed his being. With that strength came peace, joy and love crashing upon him as a tidal wave! Many were waiting to greet him. First in line was a man of great stature.

"You..." the thief stammered with amazement as the man smiled warmly at him. "You are Abraham!"

"I am," Abraham laughed heartily.

"But how do I know you..."

"Though we have never met?" Abraham finished the thief's thought. "That is the way things are here. God allows us to know one another as we are known by him."

"And how... am I able to feel things without a physical body?"

"On earth you had one kind of body. Here, you have another. However, as wondrous as this is, it does not compare to what awaits us at the resurrection—when God makes all things new."

At once the thief is greeted by the patriarchs, matriarchs and thousands of others as if he were a long lost relative dearly beloved.

"Lazarus!" the thief exclaims as a man approaches. "You are the poor beggar! Jesus spoke about you!" [48.1]

"He did," Lazarus smiles. "What a humbling moment to realize our Messiah has used me as an object lesson for so many."

"Indeed," the thief agrees. "His message that day was spread to many and eventually was told to me. At first I thought it to be a story like his other parables. But I began to wonder if it were a true picture of the reality which awaited us all. It made me think... but not enough."

"It planted a seed," Lazarus comforts, "which grew into a harvest you are now reaping."

"Yes!" the thief beams. "So, this is the Bosom of Abraham!"

"Yes," he answers. "This is the realm where God sustains the righteous—those who trust in him. Yet we are unable to enter God's direct Presence in heaven until atonement has been fully rendered."

"Atonement..." the thief remembers as he turns to Abraham. "Jesus! I saw him on the cross next to me! He is the one who came to take away the sins of the world!"

"Yes!" Abraham nods. "God's Son has paid a price we could never pay."

"Where is he? He said I would be with him..."

"You are with him," Abraham answers. "His Presence is here with us all. Through the Holy Spirit, which permeates this place, we experience our Heavenly Father and the Son."

"I do... feel... him," the thief smiles with a nod.

"And soon, he will usher us into the direct Presence of our Father."

"When will that be?"

"When he has concluded his mission of salvation for the world."

"But he died," the thief exclaims! "I saw him die with my own eyes."

"Yes, he did," Abraham agrees. "Our Heavenly Father allowed us to see the very moment. We watched with the angels and marveled at the mystery of why God would become human in order to die for us all. But, thankfully, our marveling does not dictate the counsel of our Father's Will. That... he reserves for himself. Besides... the end of the matter is not yet. Christ has died, but he must conquer death and rise again!"

The thief looks off in the distance. "And what of those who do not believe?"

"Like the thief who suffered with you?" Abraham inquires. "They are isolated in darkness and flames—separated from us by a great gulf which no one can cross. In that place it is torment and suffering: everything Christ came to save us from. But the decision which determines whether we experience paradise or torment must be made while we are still alive on earth." []

ΑΩ

❏ On Earth, Mary and Martha are in hiding along with the other disciples. Their distress and anxiety has made it difficult to sleep. Although physically and emotionally exhausted, they cannot keep their minds off of Jesus. Peter and the other disciples guard the doors with the utmost care. They are sure the Romans will come for them too, if they find out where they are. Then they could also face crucifixion. If they are discovered, most hope for a quick death at the edge of the sword. But, at the moment, that is of little importance to the women as they quietly converse in the corner of the room.

"We should go to the tomb," Mary urges.

"We cannot travel," Martha replies. "It is the Sabbath."

"The Sabbath rules never stopped Jesus."

"We are not Jesus. He moved with a purpose beyond mere rules."

"And so do we!" Mary exclaims. "I just want to know that his tomb is still secure... that his body... is safe."

"Well, don't you think I want to know that too?" Martha counters. "You don't think I want to rush out of that door with you and run to the tomb?"

They stare at each other with searching eyes.

"One more day Mary, and then we both can see. But not now."

"You are afraid."

"As we all should be! What if the Roman soldiers capture us? What if our own Jewish leaders or the temple police catch us? What then? Let us wait until the Sabbath is complete. Let us pray that all is as it should be. Then in the morning, we will go to the tomb and give our master's body a proper burial."

"But, who will roll the stone away for us?"

"I don't know."

"I… I really believed he was our Messiah…"

"As did I…"

They both weep for several moments.

"What do we do?" Mary asks.

Martha hesitates. "I wish I knew."

The evening settles on the land as the sun sets and the shadows shroud the tomb. With the night comes the cold air. Three Roman soldiers build a large fire to keep themselves warm, as they are torn between carefully guarding their posts and finding some distractions to help them pass the time. Their weapons lay against a nearby tree. The large stone still seals the entrance. In between their jesting, the guards make small talk as the fire blazes before them.

"I have never seen it like this," the first admits as he warms his hands by the fire.

"Like what?" the second soldier asks.

"Since yesterday, the wind does not blow. The birds do not chirp. Everything is silent. It is as if the world is waiting to see the outcome of the third day."

"You are talking nonsense," the third soldier scoffs. "No one rises from the dead. Not even our emperors."

"And no one," the second solder interjects, "is going to steal the criminal's body from this tomb while we are guarding it and then claim he has risen from the dead." The two soldiers laugh as the other sits quietly staring at the giant stone covering the entrance of the tomb.

"But, what if he is who he claimed to be?"

"He's dead!" the other soldier yells with finality. "He's been dead for two days and he will be dead tomorrow and every day after that!"

"And if you don't be quiet about all of this," the other soldier cackles, "we might help you join him!"

Again the soldiers laugh before growing quiet. Soon the first soldier breaks the silence. "But the centurion who was at the cross when he died... right after the earthquake... I heard him say that this man was the Son of God."

"What does that even mean?" the second soldier responds. "Being in an earthquake will make you say strange things."

"Doesn't matter. When tomorrow comes and the criminal is still dead, that will be the end of all your crazy talk. Then we can move to the next assignment. But right now, let's eat. I'm starving."

And so, the second day and night passed without incident. ◻

AΩ

◻ In the Realm of Shadows, the third day approaches. There is no movement within the tomb. Death and the Grave are secure. But things are not what they seem. Mere seconds into the third day something begins to happen.

Fallen angels stand guard at the Gates of Hell. In the far distance, a faint mist begins to form and makes its way from the east. The guards are oblivious to its near invisibility as it passes their position. This Sentient Wind gains entrance and flows down the main corridor and around corners. It descends many dark levels, passing multiple guarded stations undetected, until it comes face to face with the vaulted tomb. There... it hovers before the door... just as it hovered over the deep waters before creating life on Earth.

The Prince of Darkness, sitting on his throne is suddenly agitated. He senses something... someone familiar... yet foreign. He leaps from his perch and makes his way through the corridors of Hell, pushing past demons to find Legion. "We have an intruder!"

Legion instantly splits into six thousand versions of itself and searches all levels. Its response is almost immediate. "All areas are secure, my Lord."

Nervous energy swells within the Dark Lord. "Death!" he roars. A burst of dark energy emanates in front of him as the Death Angel appears. "My Lord?"

"Something is not right," Satan barks.

"I sense nothing—"

"Do not tell me what you sense!" Satan cuts him off. "I am Lord of this Realm!"

"I assure you, my Lord… all souls who are destined are constrained within."

"All souls…" Satan trembles. "The tomb! Summon the Grave to the tomb!"

Lucifer arrives almost instantly, with the solitary key dangling around his neck. The sight before him instills a piercing terror he has not felt since his eviction from Heaven.

"It is the third day!" he utters with a tremble in his voice, "The Spirit has come! Summon reinforcements now!"

"But Lord, you alone have the key," the Grave responds.

"Do as I command! We haven't much time!"

Hovering before the vaulted tomb, the Presence of the Holy Spirit begins to expand and reshape over the contours of the door. The Accuser glares in horror as his army of fallen angels arrive. All shudder at the sight.

"This cannot be!" Lucifer exclaims as his anger builds. "I have beaten you! The Son of God is mine!"

"I assure you," the Grave Angel speaks, "that door is impregnable! Even I cannot enter without the key you alone possess!"

The evil hordes of Satan stand as witnesses to the Presence of the Living God, as it begins to seep through the very substance, which makes up the door of the tomb! Evil begins to turn on itself as the Spirit of the Almighty permeates and penetrates the dark void within the vaulted tomb—leaving behind fine, but definite cracks in the entry, faintly resembling the shape of the very cross on which the Son of God was crucified.

The Spirit descends into the heart of oblivion. Within the vast tomb not constricted by time and space, an eternity seems to pass. The utter silence is deafening and the absence of light is blinding. But the Spirit moves with increasing momentum as the light of its very Presence illuminates its path.

Soon, it finds its mark. In front of it drifts the lifeless soul of the Son of God, fully consumed by the throes of Death. In an instant—the Spirit penetrates the dead soul of Christ.

The caverns around Satan rumble as he cries out, "This cannot be!" The vaulted tomb shakes as the Prince of Darkness perceives it to be at the epicenter of this disturbance. "No!" he yells as light pierces the tomb from the inside out.

The Death Angel screams, "Prepare for battle!" Every dark spirit stands in defiance, with their weapons ready, roaring a battle cry with ear-splitting intensity. But their yells are immediately quenched by the Son of the Living God, whose voice resounds like infinite thunder and rolls like a million waves crashing the sea.

"I AM THE RESURRECTION AND THE LIFE!"

"I AM THE RESURRECTION AND THE LIFE!!"

"I AM THE RESURRECTION AND THE LIFE!!!

In an instant, the light of his glory pierces through the dark void as the vaulted door explodes into innumerable shards! There stands the Son of Man—hovering just above the surface, radiating brighter than all the stars of the cosmos! The Christ, God's Chosen One, moves effortlessly out of the tomb to confront his enemy.

"Attack!!!" Lucifer commands as the hordes of Hell launch their most decisive and coordinated assault. But with a single thought, the Son of God repels them all! With an open hand, the keys held by Death and the Grave loose from their possession and hurtle through the cavern, landing in the strong grasp of Jesus.

"OH, DEATH, WHERE IS YOUR STING? OH, GRAVE, WHERE IS YOUR VICTORY?"[49]

The Accuser stands defiant, painfully bearing the brunt of Christ's glory. The light is more blinding than he remembers and radiates from the Son of God with such tremendous force that it takes all of the Dragon's concentration just to remain upright. Christ raises his right hand once again and the last key to all tombs rises from Lucifer's neck. The chain snaps as it flies across the cavern and settles gently within Christ's firm grip.

"Noooo!!! I Will Not Yield!" Lucifer transforms into his true form, growing instantly into a hideous monstrosity that almost fills the entire cavern. Christ is dwarfed by the size of the Dragon, as he spews prideful verbal attacks. "You will kneel before me, Son of God!"

As Satan rains down his most ferocious blow, Christ whispers a single word.

"Enough." The Presence of his glory bursts forth like a supernova, knocking the Dragon a great distance away.

Lucifer lies in a burning heap, motionless, except for his essence reverting back to its smaller form. Jesus approaches, still hovering as he passes the crater in which his fallen creation lies. As Lucifer regains consciousness, Christ pauses momentarily to declare, "I am come to destroy your works. The day of your final judgment will soon be at hand."

Lucifer looks up at Christ from the crater. "How did you..." he mumbles, wracked with pain. "You were mine..."

"You had my soul," Jesus replies firmly, "But my Father kept my Spirit for this very moment."

"But Death..." Lucifer replies. "...Nothing has ever defeated it."

Jesus stares intently at his fallen creation. "There are still things you will never understand."

Then—in the hearing of fallen angels and tormented rebellious human souls—Christ proclaims his triumphal victory throughout Satan's kingdom. Once concluded, in a flash of glory, the Master vanishes from the realm of torment and darkness and appears a great distance away... in Paradise. [49.1] ⬚

AΩ

☐ *An immense glory marks Jesus' sudden arrival in Paradise as the angels, who have been assigned to serve the righteous begin shouting his praises. Both angels and humans converge upon their Lord as jubilation breaks forth! In this realm not limited by time and space, Jesus greets all as if they are the only ones present—including the thief.*

"My Lord and my God!" the thief rejoices as he hugs Jesus. "You remembered me as I asked!"

"Yes," Jesus laughs warmly. "And now you have been with me here in Paradise! Are you ready for what is next!"

"Yes, my Lord," the thief laughs. "I will go wherever you tell me!"

"On earth you were known by many as a thief," Jesus declares, "but now you will be known—like all humans here are known—as one who has been redeemed by me."

Jesus steps back from the crowd as several angels draw near. "My brothers and sisters! You who have waited here in Paradise for the fulfillment of the Atonement. All has been secured! Enter into the joy of our Heavenly Father!"

With the wave of his hand, an enormous portal opens before them. They watch in amazement as heaven is revealed in all of its unmitigated glory! Angels await on the other side of the portal, welcoming each as they begin to cross over from Paradise. Jesus gazes at his sisters and brothers with great joy as they enter into the direct presence of his Father. Moments later, the patriarchs and matriarchs approach.

"Lord," they inquire. "Are you not coming?"

"Not yet," Jesus smiles warmly. "I must first take up my body from the tomb on earth. Then you will see me.[50] ☐

ΑΩ

Here we are—the finite trying to understand the infinite and eternal…

Such is the nature of Death… until this very moment it had been impregnable. Unstoppable. Irrevocable. An impending doom to which there was no escape. Victorious. Voracious. Always consuming and never satisfied. The antithesis of life eternal. Darker than darkness.

More menacing than a black hole in its efficacy to strip all light, life, and consciousness from the very souls of its victims.

It stood opposed to God from before the beginning of time; as if a realm all its own refusing to be conquered. And so, it was directed; like a mighty wave which can't be stopped, it was swayed into obedience. As a rabid animal, which can't be tamed, it was forced by the hand of God in service to his bidding. And whenever God pulled back his power, Death would swoop in like air filling a vacuum and like darkness infiltrating an area where the absence of light had occurred; and it swallowed whole all life in its path.

While on earth, Christ could command it to release its cold grip on individuals. But it would always return to ravage all life once more. Until this day... when it would be defeated once and for all. And how did Christ prevail? You see, that is the mystery. What is sure, is that Death, with all of its power and authority, had one weakness. But even Death did not know of its existence. Neither did that fallen guardian cherub who is known by many names, which held and manipulated its power. Until this day, none had ever been powerful enough to *free themselves* from its grip.

But God in his infinite wisdom knew of this weakness; most likely even placed it there. Death could only be defeated from the inside out. And Christ is the only one who had been given power to overcome God's greatest enemy! In the ultimate act of submission and sacrifice, Christ gave himself to be consumed by this enemy that causes all people to tremble in fear. Death had always been the hunter, but it had now become the prey. Death had always been the conqueror, but it had now been overcome by the One who was *more* than a Conqueror. Hebrews 2:14-15 puts it this way:

"Since the children have flesh and blood, he too shared in their humanity so that by his death he might break the power of him who holds the power of death—that is, the devil—and free those who all their lives were held in slavery by their fear of death."

Death was no longer the final outcome. Christ had obliterated it so that humanity would no longer fear death of the body, nor death of the soul. For those who believed in Christ, death—in all of its forms—no longer was of any consequence! It had been reduced to a mere doorway that a human walked through at the end of his or her earthly life, which led to the Presence of God. All that death could and would steal, Christ would reverse on the last day through the resurrection. And this reversal would be unending.

God was in Christ, single-handedly defeating sin and death in order to reconcile the world to himself. And in a magnificent and ultimate act of creation, God did something in Christ which is unfathomable. Christ, the eternal Son of God, allowed himself to be consumed by death. Then, through the process of the resurrection, Jesus Christ *became* something he had never been! He became the Firstborn over all creation. The Firstborn of the dead. The Firstborn among many brothers and sisters. His body forever changed from corruptible to incorruptible; at once both physical and spiritual. And we who believe shall be like him!

And the day will come when the realm of Death will be destroyed for all eternity. Never to be heard of again. Death will become a distant memory, which will fade away into nothingness. All that will remain is LIFE ETERNAL in all of its fullness. And God will be all… in all.[51]

PART THREE

RESURRECTION!

MINUTES BEFORE THE SUN'S RAYS WAKE THE CITY OF JERUSALEM ON THE THIRD DAY, THE GROUND AROUND THE TOMB WHERE THE BODY OF JESUS LIES BURIED BEGINS TO TREMBLE. The Roman soldiers stare in disbelief as they notice a sudden flash of light piercing through the small spaces between the massive rock and the tomb's entrance. And then… nothing.

Inside the tomb, the badly beaten body of Jesus begins to completely heal itself. Seconds later, Jesus breathes deeply as the ceremonial burial cloth falls away from him. He opens his eyes and stares into the darkness for a moment as he feels the surge of the Spirit infusing and transforming every cell of his body. He reaches up with both hands and removes the cloth which lay across his face. His diaphragm quivers and a slight chuckle escapes his lips.

Still lying down, Jesus takes a good stretch, like one would do in the morning after waking up from a long night's sleep. He inhales deeply, running his fingers through his hair, and presses his now warm hands against the cold stone slab before sitting up and then standing to his feet. He then carefully folds the facial cloth and places it next to where his head had been lying. He does all this in the dark, yet to his eyes, even the darkness is full of light.[52]

Meanwhile, outside the tomb, lightning flashes across the sky. Thunder bellows as the wind picks up. The clouds rip open. An angel, terrifying in stature and glory, descends to the earth. The Roman soldiers stare in a speechless panic as the angel lands in between them and the tomb.

"Sleep!" the angel commands, and the soldiers fall to the ground as dead men—their swords and shields clanging on the hard surface.

As the sun rises above the horizon, the angel rolls the massive stone away, with a mighty arm, as if it were a pebble. There stands Jesus, smiling, with a twinkle in his eye. The angel bows low, worshiping him, his hands upraised. "My Lord and my God!"

Jesus steps out of the tomb, his bare feet touching the cool, moist soil. He approaches the angel and places his hand on his right shoulder. "Well done," he says warmly.

"You are the Lord of all creation," the angel acknowledges.

Jesus smiles approvingly and beckons the angel to stand. The risen Christ takes a panoramic view of his creation. Several birds fly to him and land on his outstretched hands, chirping new songs. Jesus laughs heartily, the wind blowing through his hair.

"Beautiful, aren't they?"

The angel nods, "They are, my Lord."

"Everything seems more vibrant!" Jesus declares as he launches the birds into the air and watches them fly away. "Oh, how I've missed the colors!"

The angel smiles.

"And you," Jesus continues, "You were created for this very hour... It is good to be back in this world... What was stolen from humanity has been redeemed. Now, I must prepare my disciples for the task which lies ahead. They will continue what I have begun, and out of every tribe and nation on Earth a new eternal family will be brought forth—fashioned from the old. Through me all things will be made new. All power in heaven and on earth is now mine. I grant my power freely to those who believe in me, so that the works I have done—they will do, and even greater because I will shortly return to my Father."[53]

Both Christ and the angel turn at the same time. "They are coming," Jesus says, looking in the direction of a distant tree line. "When they arrive, give them the message. Then return to your brothers and tell them what you have seen and heard. I am sure they have many questions. I will follow shortly."

"Yes, my Lord," the angel responds as Jesus vanishes from sight.

Mary Magdalene and several other women fight to hold back their tears as they make their way through the garden to the tomb. With each step their breathing becomes more labored. Suddenly, as if on cue, the women stop crying. Their eyes widen at the sight before them.

"No..." Mary mumbles as she breaks into a run toward the open tomb.

Once at the tomb, they find an angel sitting on top of the stone that had been rolled away.

His countenance was like lightning as he spoke. "Do not be afraid, for I know that you seek Jesus who was crucified. He is not here; for he is risen, as he said. Come, see the place where the Lord did lay. And go quickly. Tell his disciples that he is risen from the dead, and indeed he is going before you into Galilee; there you will see him. Behold, I have told you." In a flash, the angel was gone. The women ran back to their homes. While they were gone, the three soldiers awoke and ran away. Then Mary returned with Peter and John. Both disciples looked in the tomb. Unsure what to make of things, they ran off in silence.

But Mary stayed and wept... overwhelmed by the unexpected news and by the fact that Jesus was nowhere to be found. Did she really see an angel? Was what she heard true? Or was she so distraught that her mind had made it all up? As she knelt, someone approached from behind.

"Woman, why are you weeping?"

Startled, she turns around, wiping her eyes and nose. "Are you the grounds keeper?" She asks between sobs and sniffles. Her view of him blurred by her tears as sunlight radiates from behind him.

"Who are you looking for?" the man responds.

"Sir, if you have moved his body, please tell me where my master is and I will retrieve him."

"Mary!" the man calls out warmly. Immediately she knew!

"Teacher!" She runs to him and throws herself at his feet. "You are alive!"

"Do not cling to me," Jesus says. "I first must ascend to my Father. But go! Tell my brethren I am ascending to my Father and your Father, and to my God and your God. Tell them I will see them soon!"[54]

Like a world-class sprinter, Mary takes off, grabbing her flowing garments in one hand. She had never run so fast and so far in her life! But she had been given the most amazing message of all and her heart was bursting with excitement! She had to tell the others! Jesus did in fact live! He was alive! And she had seen him with her own eyes, heard him with her own ears and touched him with her own hands! Death did not conquer him! He was alive! ◻

AΩ

◻ Jesus waited until Mary had gone. He gazed again at his creation. It was pleasing in his sight. But there was one thing left to do to complete the Divine-Human transaction. "Father," he whispered, "I am coming."

In an instant, the Son of God appeared high above the planet—floating in Earth's orbit. No longer needing to breathe oxygen, he smiled before turning around to face the expanse of the universe. Within moments he eagerly began to fly through the dark, cold void of space. His arms were opened wide and his face shined brighter than the sun!

With a smile he blazed through the cosmos, moving faster than light itself, as the very fabric of space and time fluxed around him. Even at this incredible speed, he took in each moment as if it were the only moment. It was as if the universe paused in humble submission to its Creator. The heavens declared his glory as he passed stars and planets, asteroid belts and nebulae, quasars, galaxies and a host of celestial bodies.[55] Each resonated at its own frequency—creating a symphony of music only he could hear. His laughter grew with each passing second. Then, in a flash of brilliance, as Jesus neared the boundary of the known universe, he exited time and space altogether... ◻

AΩ

◻ A symphony a music—similar to trumpets—can be heard as the Gates of Heaven open. Angels, saints, and other heavenly citizens eagerly line both sides of the Street of Gold. They cheer loudly as Christ enters and makes his way towards the Throne Room. Jesus waves to the crowd, but he suddenly stops in front of a man—the thief from the cross—and they embrace. Word had already spread from the angel who had rolled the stone away. All of Heaven rejoices at their triumphant King and at what the Father, Son, and the Holy Spirit have accomplished!

As Jesus draws close to the entrance of the Throne Room, he can hear the voices of the four living creatures crying out: "Holy, holy, holy is the Lord God Almighty! Who was, is and is to come!"[56] He ascends the great staircase as the angels who stand guard bow their heads in reverence before opening the massive triune entry to God's Throne. Even with the glory which already fills heaven, a bright light—with a unique glory all its own—bursts forth through the open doors.

Jesus enters among the Seraphim, Cherubim, the twenty-four Elders and the four Living Creatures. All who are present engage in worshiping the Triune One. The Seraphim and Cherubim cry out: "Holy, holy, holy is the Lord of hosts! The whole earth is full of your glory!" As Jesus makes his way to the Throne, the twenty-four elders kneel, casting their golden crowns at his feet.[57]

"MY SON!" The words reverberate through the atmosphere of the Throne Room. They come from the One who sits on the Throne in unapproachable light. Lightning and rolling thunders echo his words.

"FATHER!" Jesus rejoices as he ascends the majestic steps and walks into the blazing Presence of the Ancient of Days. The Holy Spirit fills the temple and wraps Himself around the Father and the Son as the Triune Godhead fellowships as One once again.

After some time, the Son of God exits his Father's glory and proceeds to the mercy seat before the altar. There, Jesus sprinkles his blood upon it.[58]

With a broad smile of victory he proclaims: "This is the New Covenant in my blood. The final task is complete. Redemption has been secured for all who will believe in me. Power to become the children of God and to live this new life has been made available. Satan, Sin, Hell, Death and the Grave have been conquered. The Father will soon send the Holy Spirit." ▯

AΩ

Within God lives this mystery of the Trinity—THREE yet ONE. All the same essence, yet with unique authority. We must wait until eternity, when we see God face to face before we can even hope to fully understand. Even then, we may still not. But until then, let us embrace the mystery of our triune God, who has given us life eternal…

AΩ

❑ During the evening of Christ's resurrection, the disciples were huddled in a house. The windows were shut. The doors were locked. They were terrified at the prospect of being found by the authorities. All they could do was debate about what Mary and the other women claimed they saw.[59]

"It could not have been Jesus. We saw him dead with our own eyes!"

"But I saw him alive," Mary counters.

"I don't believe it."

"And even if what you said was true," another disciple adds, "why would the angel tell women and not Peter and John? We all know according to Jewish law the testimonies of women are not credible."

"But, what they said is true," two other disciples countered. "Early this afternoon, we were walking on the road to Emmaus when Jesus appeared to us. We didn't recognize him at first. He looked different somehow."[60]

"That's because it wasn't him!" another disciple interrupts. "It was just someone who resembled him!"

"But then," the disciples continue, "he opened up the Scriptures to us and our hearts burned as he spoke."

"Bah!" A disciple retorts. "That was nothing more than indigestion! How do you know it was him?"

"We asked him to stay and eat with us. At the table he took bread, broke it, and blessed it. It was then that our eyes were opened and we knew it was him. Then he vanished from our sight!"

"You both were hallucinating. It wasn't him."

"Well, ask Peter and John. They went to the tomb."

The group turns and looks at them, still filled with doubt.

"So, what do you two think? Is Jesus alive?"

Peter and John stare at each other in silence and then at the group.

"We don't know."

Just then, the disciples yell in fright as Jesus appears among them and declares, "Peace be with you."

The men stagger backwards, holding each other tightly, their wild expressions registering their true thoughts. "It's a ghost!"

Mary Magdalene stands and smiles. Jesus returns her smile with a nod as he turns and faces the men.

"Why are you all so quick to disbelieve?" Jesus rebukes them softly. "Even with proof from eye witnesses you resist. Did you not remember what I said before my death?"

"That you would rise on the third day after you died," John answers.

"Master," James asks, "Is it really... you?"

Jesus smiles and extends his arms toward them. "Come and see."

The men and women make their way across the room to Jesus, embracing him and lovingly touching the nail prints in his hands and feet.

"Do the scars... hurt?"

"Not anymore," he smiles. "It is me. Do you have any fish?"

The men laugh at his request as their fear slowly melts away.

"We... we have so many questions."

"There will be time for that," Jesus answers. "Right now, let's share a meal together. I need to eat something. Don't you?"

During the meal, Jesus encourages them from the Scriptures and ends with a declaration.

"As our Father has sent me… so I now send you. Receive the Holy Spirit." Then Jesus breathed on them. [61] []

ΑΩ

Thomas, who was one of the disciples, was not with the rest when Jesus first appeared. Eight days later, they were still trying to convince him that they had in fact seen Jesus alive.

"Just shut up!" Thomas snapped. "All of this foolishness. I will *not* believe unless I see him with my own eyes and place my fingers in the nail prints and my hand in his side!"

Eight days later, when they were all together in the locked home, Jesus appeared once again.

"Peace be with you!"

The disciples were ecstatic. Thomas was both frightened and skeptical.

"Thomas," Jesus said, "come and see the nail prints. Put your fingers in them. Place your hand in my side. Stop doubting and believe!"

Thomas fell to his knees and cried out, "My Lord and my God!"

Jesus smiled as he placed his hand on Thomas' head. He gazed at him with eyes full of kindness. "You believe because you see me with your own eyes… Even more blessed are those who will believe in me without having ever seen me with their physical eyes."[62]

ΑΩ

Jesus stayed in Jerusalem for forty days. More than five hundred witnesses saw him and he performed many signs and wonders to prove to them that he had in fact risen from the dead. He produced so many signs, that multiple volumes of a book could not contain them all.[63]

At the end of the forty days, Jesus and his disciples trekked to the top of the mountain known as the Mount of Olives. While on the journey, his disciples asked if he would now usher in his kingdom on earth.

"It is not for you to know the times or seasons for what you have asked. The Father has put this event under his authority alone."

A few minutes later he continued…

"Remember what I have already said to you. In my Father's house are many mansions; if it were not so, I would have told you. I am going away to prepare a place for you and all who will believe. When it is done, I will come again and receive you all to myself; so that you will be with me."

Christ then commissioned his disciples to go and take his message to the world.

"All authority has been given to me in heaven and earth. Go! Make disciples of all nations, baptizing them in the name of the Father and of the Son and of the Holy Spirit. Teach those who believe to observe all of the things I have commanded you. And know, I am with you always, even until the end of the age."

The disciples were amazed and filled with excitement for what the future would bring! They were ready to run! But there was one thing they needed to do first:

"Wait in Jerusalem for the Promise of the Father," Jesus said. "Not many days from now, you will receive power when the Holy Spirit has come upon you; and you will be witnesses to me beginning in Jerusalem and spreading to the end of the earth."

Having said these words to his disciples, Jesus smiled, raised his arms and rose straightway into the sky. The disciples watched in awe as he ascended. Moments later, they squinted hard as Jesus pierced the clouds and could no longer be seen. Just then, two angels appeared wearing white robes which radiated like the sun.

"Men of Galilee, why do you stand here gazing up to the sky? This same Jesus you just saw ascend into the clouds will return in like manner."[64]

In a flash, they were gone. The disciples stood motionless, pondering all they had seen and heard. Their Lord was alive! Their Messiah had risen from the dead! Celestial beings had punctuated the truth they had just witnessed with an explanation mark!

No doubt, the disciples wanted desperately to go with Jesus. But, he had commissioned them to a work. A necessary work, which could not be ignored. No matter the cost, others needed to hear the Good News.

Everyone needed to know that God had paid the debt for their sin and provided an eternal home for them through his Son! Even if they didn't realize or think they needed it or even deserved it, it *was* true. Eternal Life was now available to all who believed.

After some time on the mountain, these men and women returned to Jerusalem and gathered in the appointed upper room. There, they began to pray for the promise Jesus declared would soon come from God, the Father. And there they worshiped Jesus, for everything he had done.

PART FOUR

THE PROMISE FULFILLED

NOT MANY DAYS LATER, THE PROMISE BECAME REALITY AS THE HOLY SPIRIT FELL ON 120 FOLLOWERS OF JESUS. They were gathered together in prayer in an upper room in Jerusalem on the Day of Pentecost. Like a mighty rushing wind the Spirit of God entered the room in a visible, audible, tangible form! The Fire of God's Presence—as was on the bush in Moses' day—swirled above their heads and then split into individual flames and rested on each follower.[65]

If your eyes were opened to the spiritual realm, you would have seen 120 humans begin to blaze in glory as the Fire of God filled their entire being. If you had been there, perhaps, your mind would have reflected on the words of Jesus, "The kingdom of God is within you."[66]

This explosion of God's Spirit upon the world ushered in the birth of the Ecclesia—those who have been called out from the world into the family of God—those Born Again from above. On that day, the gospel of God's kingdom was declared by Peter to thousands and 3,000 people placed their faith in Jesus Christ as the Son of God! In that instant they became citizens of Heaven as they were regenerated—made new—by the Holy Spirit.[67]

Down through each generation, this new heavenly family of God continued to grow and it still grows today! The evidence of this new reality is first found in the Bible, and then in the countless stories of millions who have been transformed by an encounter with Jesus Christ. People from across the globe—from every ethnicity, class, and economic background; from upstanding citizens to dissidents to the worst criminals ever imagined. They have been redeemed by the One who is both the Lamb of God who takes away the sin of the world and the Lion of Judah who is the victorious King! This radical transformation of the heart and mind has brought about some of the greatest contributions to human societies and cultures since Christ walked the earth. Truly, those who lived in darkness have seen God's *great* shining light![68]

"Yet to all who did received him, to those who believed in his name, he gave the right to become children of God—children born not of natural descent, nor of human decision or a husband's will, but born of God." —John 1: 12-13

God has adopted us into his holy and royal family! Through Christ we have become joint-heirs of God's inheritance for his children, as well as a royal priesthood. This is what God desires: **to conform those of us who believe into the image of his Son, that Christ may be the firstborn among many brethren.** Jesus Christ is not only King of all kings, he is also our Elder Brother![69]

ΑΩ

This brings us to an inconvenient truth: **before Christ returns to usher in his kingdom, the war we have been born into must play out.** Since there are those who have received Christ, there are also those who reject him and truly despise all that Jesus represents. These persons go out of their way in an attempt to destroy the church and anything that represents truth. This will eventually lead to a time of great tribulation, which the world has yet to know. Christ spoke of the signs that would herald the beginning of the end:

"Be careful that no one deceives you. Many will come in my name, claiming, 'I am the Christ,' and will deceive countless many. And you will hear of wars and rumors of wars. Do not be troubled; because all of these things must come to pass, but the end is not yet. Nations will rise against each other and kingdoms will rage against one another. Famines, pestilence and earthquakes will ravage the earth. All these things are the beginning of sorrows.

"A great falling away will happen as you are delivered into tribulation and are killed and hated just because you belong to me. Then many will be offended and will betray each other and hatred will cause much violence.

"Many false prophets will rise causing rampant deception. Because of overwhelming lawlessness the love of many will grow cold. But those who endure to the end will be saved. And this gospel of my Kingdom will be proclaimed throughout the entire world as a witness to all the nations, and then the end will come."[70]

ΑΩ

And then the end will come…

Do the words of Christ sound familiar to you? We see many of these things beginning to happen with increasing frequency. There's an increase in wars and rumors of wars; in kingdoms and nations raging against one another; and in natural disasters. Even within the last twenty years there have been a number of men around the world who have claimed to be Jesus Christ. They have amassed followers in the thousands. Deception is also on the rise as false teachings abound. The world seems poised for the fulfillment of these words as humanity heads down a path towards self-annihilation.

However, at some point, before the world self-destructs, humanity will rally around a charismatic ruler. Peace and prosperity will come to the Middle East and to the rest of the world as a new world order will be established. At this point, it will seem like Earth has been turned into utopia as national boundaries and distinctions will become almost non-existent. The masses will laud the ruler and will pledge allegiance to him by taking a mark on their bodies.

This "mark of the beast" will be a technological implant that will allow the user passage and privilege in the world's new economy. But the masses either won't know or won't care that Lucifer himself is influencing this world leader. However, it will become absolutely clear when this person walks into Jerusalem's third temple and declares himself "to be God" and will demand that he be worshiped as such. This leader is known as the Anti-Christ and will be used as one of the Dragon's last attempts at rebellion against God. He will deceive the entire world and turn creation against the Creator.

But utopia will morph into a dystopia after the Anti-Christ has been assassinated and comes back to life. However, it will not be the leader who returns to life, but Lucifer himself who will inhabit his body, playing him like a puppet—just as he did the serpent back in the Garden of Eden. Peace will give way to turmoil as the great tribulation begins. This will be a time of testing that the people of Earth have never experienced before. This will be a 3.5-year period of great worldwide persecution. Anyone who chooses not to side with the new world regime will be in grave danger—especially Jews and quite possibly Christians.

NOTE: *I say "quite possibly" because there are those who believe the church will experience this time of tribulation (at least partially). Others believe God will rapture the church away from Earth before the tribulation takes place. Either way, let our faith be in Christ alone, whether we are raptured before the tribulation begins or during this time of suffering. (I write more about this in the appendix article: The Rapture).*

The Anti-Christ will be worse than any dictator who has ruled in history. He will position himself to be worshiped by all and will rally humanity against God and his people. There will be death in the streets, natural disasters around the world, and astronomical signs in the skies. These incidents are meant to call humanity to repentance, but many will be too caught up in the frenzy and will choose to remain enemies of God. Then the largest war the earth has ever known will take place as humanity "shakes its fist in the air" in opposition to their Creator's rightful rule. Then, Jesus Christ, the King of Glory will return and utterly defeat Lucifer and all who have followed him.[71]

AΩ

THE DAY OF JUDGMENT

"It is appointed for humans to live, die and then be judged…"[72]

At the end of time, angels will storm the earth as Jesus Christ pierces the sky. Before, Christ was the Lamb of God who came to take away the sin of humanity. Now, Jesus returns with the armies of heaven as the Conquering King who comes to judge all the earth. Every eye shall see him. Every ear will hear his voice. And no one will be able to deny the truth of his eternal existence.

Before his crucifixion, Jesus stood before the Roman governor, Pilate, who asked, "What is truth?" and in disdain walked away. If Pilate had stayed, Jesus would have replied, "I AM TRUTH," a fact everyone will realize on the day when he returns.

With one word, Christ will defeat his enemies—Lucifer, his fallen angels and all who refuse to yield to the lordship of Christ. A great angel will cast Lucifer into an Abyss, where he will be imprisoned for 1000 years. During this time, Jesus will reign on the earth. Christ will rule the entire world from Jerusalem fully demonstrating a true and righteous government. Peace will be the standard and God's glory will reign supreme. (See appendix article, Your Kingdom Come, for more information).

At the end of the thousand years, Lucifer will be released from the Abyss to make one last desperate attempt to disrupt God's sovereignty. His scheme to rally the inhabitants of the earth against their Creator will prove futile and then his final judgment will commence! That great dragon who deceived the whole world, the accuser of the brethren, the enemy of our souls, the false god of this world, Satan, the devil, the corrupter, the father of lies, the adversary to everything God willed to do in all creation—will have nowhere to run and will be rendered completely powerless before our Holy Creator. Then he will be thrown into the lake of fire. This is the second death: a fiery oblivion of eternal torment, anguish, and separation from God's Presence.

☐ *An unmeasurable expanse resting before the great white throne of God...*

Lucifer stands before God's throne bound in restraints. Three strong archangels guard him. His visage is defiant—yet he is utterly defeated. Around him are a myriad of witnesses—angels and saints of God—watching the final outcome of evil.

"So, this day has finally arrived," Lucifer sputters. "My time of judgment."

"For millenniums," God declares, "you who have been known by many names—have rebelled against me and all that is good which I have created."

"But would you destroy me without cause?" Lucifer questions. "Are you afraid

to let those present hear the truth about who you really are?"

A saint stares in astonishment as she looks at an angel near her and asks, "How can he talk like that to God?"

"It is his nature," the angel answers. "As is our Creator's nature to allow him. Our God always speaks and acts from the position of victory."

"Your condemnation is sure," God replies, "but you may state your case for all to hear. It is the nature of evil to blind both its victims and those who seek to control it, from the truth."

"I am not blind!" Lucifer roars. "I now see clearer than ever! You are a tyrant! You have always been one! You force your will on all creation! And I have fought to free creation from your wrath!"

"I Am that I Am. I do not change. I Am Good. Loving. All-Powerful. All-Knowing. You are, in fact, the tyrant. My motives are always pure and right."

"Your motives are pure?" Lucifer balks. "You have always held back the choicest things for yourself!"

"As Creator of all—that is my prerogative. But I do not merely reserve the choicest things; all things are reserved for me and for my pleasure."

"But that is not right!" Lucifer shouts as the angels and saints look on.

"That is where you have erred," God replies. "You, Lucifer, were the highest of my angelic creation. Pure and perfect in all of your ways. Yet you chose, with your free will, to believe something other than truth."

"But you gave me my will! Now you will damn me to eternal torment for using it? Why not make me and my brothers like the robots your wretched humans create?"

"I do not want mindless automatons. However, this is not your true point of contention. You chose to venture into what was forbidden—you who carried praise to me from the angels. You siphoned praise for yourself and that choice began your perversion."

"I am as good as you!" Lucifer roars. "I deserve to be praised and worshiped *as you are!"*

"All created things produce praise and worship in their own way. Since all things are reserved for me, only I am capable of receiving praise and worship as it was intended to be. If given to anyone else, praise and worship produces in them pride, as it did in you."

"But you knew that! And still you did nothing to warn me of the danger!"

"You knew very well that all praise and worship is mine. That in itself is warning enough."

"But you could have stopped me before it happened! You know all things!"

"Yes. I could have stopped you from stealing the praise and worship which was due me. I could have also stopped you from appropriating and unleashing a dark power which you did not truly understand."

"But you didn't! So all of this is **your** fault! The pain, suffering, murder, war, hatred, greed, lies, rebellion—**you** are to blame! Not me!"

"Even now, you place blame other than where it truly resides. You fail to take responsibility for your own actions, which has led you down this path. I freely give and act according to the counsel of my own will. As the Author, Sustainer and Purveyor of Life, Truth and Love, I do not react to the accusations of falsehood. I define the parameters of all truth and reality."

"But you created me to worship you. There were no other options!"

"You were a vessel of honor, until you dishonored yourself by your actions. Nor did you trust me to wait and see the final outcome of my intended purpose for you."

"Your intended purpose?" Lucifer balks. "Your intended purpose for me and my brothers is replacement! You chose to create the humans because we weren't good enough for you!"

"Again, you have been blinded by your own pride and arrogance. Both angels and humans hold a significant place within the counsel of my will. But you will never know where their paths lead because your path diverges at this point."

"At least I have corrupted your wretched humans!" Lucifer snickers. "A countless number of them will be joining me in oblivion!"

"That," God replies solemnly, "is the only solace you will have. Yet, it will not be enough to quell the torment which awaits you. Even in your rebellion, I have worked all things for my glory. For all things work together for the good of those who love me and are called according to my purpose."

"How can you say you are a God of love, yet you allowed all this to happen? How can you say you are just, if you take the humans to yourself but will not receive me and my brothers back into your presence?"

"I AM the Supreme Law Giver!" the voice of God echoes powerfully throughout the great expanse. "Even now your words betray you. I see your heart. You have no desire to return to me, but only to escape what awaits you. You do not ask out of love. I do not receive you or the angels that sided with you because you rebelled with full and complete knowledge of your actions. I receive the humans to myself because they did not know what they were truly doing when they resisted me. Even now, only those humans who have received my Son will be in Our Presence. In this, justice is served."

"Your justice is nothing more than a ruse for your tyranny!"

"Again, you do not understand the true nature of love. To force my will on all at every turn, in the name of love or any other name, is in actuality tyranny. I am not a dictator. Yet, I am righteous and must judge all things. Now, Lucifer—the deceiver of the angels and the whole world—you who held the power of death for a time—your moment of judgment has now come."

The glory of God's Presence bursts forth as Lucifer is forced to his knees by the brilliance of the display. With all of his strength, he grits his teeth tightly— trying to refuse the words, which, even now, force their way into his mind. But his mouth can't remain shut as the words rise up his throat and spill from his lips.

"Jesus... is........Lord! To the glory... of... God... the Father!"

A giant portal pierces the very fabric of the expanse next to where Lucifer kneels. He falls back, terrified at the sight and sound of the roaring fire that awaits him. The three archangels grab him and position him in front of the portal as it ripples the very material of reality.

"Lucifer, you shall now be cast into the Second Death. The realms of Death and Hades will be cast into the Second Death as well. Then, all fallen angels and unrepentant humans will be cast into the Second Death. And all of you will be in torment for eternity."

Lucifer shrieks as the three archangels hurl him through the opening of the portal. His cries are drowned by the roar of the flames as the portal closes as quickly as it appeared. Now, Lucifer, who was the father of lies and the deceiver of the entire world is no more. ▯

After Satan, Death and Hades are thrown into the Second Death. Then all humans who ever lived will stand before God's Great Throne to give an account of *how* they lived.[73]

ΑΩ

▯ Billions upon billions of souls stand within a great expanse which seems to have no ending. Each wonders, "What is this place?" It is a sea of humanity in a never-ending line. Yet, each have a private audience as angels approach and various books materialize before them. Men and women, boys and girls all facing the same ultimate truth: it is appointed for each person to live, then die, then face God's judgment. All face this reality at the same time... each soul being judged at once, as if he or she were the only one present.

"Where am I?" a man asks the angel nearest to him.

"You are in the place of judgment," the angel replies.

"Is this... heaven?"

"We are just outside its realm," the angel replies as the large ancient books are opened.

"What are these books?" the man inquires.

"These are the records of all you have done while you were alive on earth."

"I… believed in God."

The angel looks at the man with piercing eyes but says nothing as the pages begin to flip open. With each turn of a page, images flash in front of them; many images he is not pleased to see. In an instant, his entire life is recounted.

"How do you plead?" the angel inquires.

"Not guilty!" the man insists. "I-I did a lot of good in my life! I helped a lot of people! Surely that counts for something!"

Suddenly, a flash of blinding light fills the atmosphere. All the humans try to shield themselves as waves of purity roll over them. Before them sits a Being on a throne that flames with raw, unadulterated power. His garment is the purest white—whiter than the freshest of snow. His long, flowing woolly hair glows. A fiery stream flows from his Throne as thousands upon thousands of angels bow in his Presence while the souls of humanity gaze in fearful wonder.

"Is that… God?" the man asks.

"Yes," the angel responds. "He is the Ancient of Days. The Creator and Sustainer of all things seen and unseen. The Judge over every realm of existence."

At once, the Ancient of Days speaks to all—at once all hear as if they are the only one present.

"How does this soul plead?"

"Not guilty," the angel answers.

"Even when confronted with Truth, you still resist," God replies.

"Please!" the man cries out. "Have mercy on me!"

"The time for mercy has passed."

"But I believed in you!"

"Even the demons believe and tremble. But, like them, you never placed your trust in my path of salvation."[74]

"Tell me what to do and I will do it!"

"You already have heard the way, but you chose not to follow the path."

"What way?" he exclaims.

"My Son."

"Jesus Christ? He was a good man, a great teacher!"

"Yet, you did not take his teachings to heart. You did not allow him to change you. If you had, I would have adopted you as one of my own. Therefore, you cannot enter my kingdom."[75]

"Please!" the man begs. "I accept him now!"

In a blinding flash of light, like the first, Jesus—The Son of Man—appears in front of the man, sitting on a glorious throne. Christ is robed in royal majesty, his eyes bright as a flaming fire, his skin glowing as polished bronze, his beard full and hair flowing; the nail prints in his hands and feet evident.

"It is too late to receive me now," Jesus declares with a mixture of sorrow and finality. "I came to you on many occasions while you were alive on Earth. Oh, how I wanted to draw you to myself, yet you were not willing. You chose to gain the whole world at the expense of your soul."[76]

"But, Lord…" the man utters as he drops to his knees.

"You call me Lord only because you finally see in death what was always available to you in life."

"You are the Son of God," the man pleads. "Surely you can let me in if you wish. Look at all the good I've done!"

"It is not about the good you've done. No one is good but God. Your sin keeps you from me. If you had received **my** goodness, then you would have been covered in my blood and your sin would have been washed away. But, even now it remains. You lived apart from me. You died apart from me. Now, you must carry the wrath of your sin for all eternity."[77]

A portal opens next to the man. Fierce fire, heat and an ominous roar emanate from the fissure.

"Jesus, please!" the man cries. "Please don't send me there!"

"I do not send you," Jesus replies. "You have sent yourself."[78]

At once the man screams as his soul is pulled into the portal and it shuts as quickly as it had appeared... []

ΑΩ

Imagine, having to answer the Righteous Judge for all you have ever said, done or thought... everything brought to light. Nothing hidden. Every secret unearthed for all to see. Every motivation weighed. Who can stand when facing such a judgment? Who wouldn't be found guilty for breaking God's holy standards? Who can do enough good to outweigh their sins? If that was even the scale God used to judge every soul. Listen to the Scriptures...[79]

"The devil, who deceived the world, was cast into the lake of fire and brimstone where the beast and the false prophet are. And they will be tormented day and night forever and ever. Then I saw a great white throne and him who sat on it, from whose face the earth and the sky fled away. And there was found no place for them. And I saw the dead, unknown and famous, standing before God, and books were opened. And another book was opened, which was the Book of Life. And the dead were judged according to their works, by the things which were written in the books. The sea gave up the dead who were in it, and Death and Hades delivered up the dead who were in them. And they were judged, each according to his works. Then Death and Hades were cast into the lake of fire. This is the second death. And anyone not found written in the Book of Life was cast into the lake of fire."[80]

AΩ

❏ *Billions more stood before Christ, the angels, and the Ancient of Days: God the Father. These were those who had placed their faith in Jesus Christ, the Son of God. The books assigned to each soul were opened—as with the others— and their lives played out before them in vivid detail. Their sins were evident before the Father. And they felt shame for missing the mark. Their works for Christ were also put on display. Even more importantly, the motivations behind the works they did were brought forth into the light.*

Each work was tried by the intense fire of God's Presence in order to test its purity. Those actions that were built on the foundation of Christ—which were done for God's glory—survived the test. But those works which were done for selfish gain, no matter how great the earthly outcome of applause and adoration, did not survive the flames and were reduced to an ash heap.[81]

"How do you plead?" God the Father asks.

Each soul replies in similar fashion, "Guilty."

And then Jesus speaks. "Father, these are the ones you gave to me. They have placed their faith in me and I have washed them with my blood. Their sins are forgiven."

The Ancient of Days opens the great Book of Life, which lists the names of every child of God… every citizen of Heaven. Within its glowing pages the names of these who were redeemed by the blood of the Lamb are found written in exquisite gold lettering. Christ declares each one with great exuberance! These billions stand from every nation, tribe, and kindred on Earth. The saints fall to their knees in spontaneous worship, with hearts overflowing with love and gratitude, as they utter, "You are LORD! You are the Son of Man who judges righteously!"

"Well done my good and faithful servants!" Jesus exclaims with outstretched hands. "You who were adopted from the foundation of the world… you who have been covered by my blood and sealed by the Holy Spirit. Through me you have been faithful over the things which were assigned for you to accomplish. Even in your failures and weakness, my grace has been sufficient. Now come! Enter the Kingdom! Enter the joy of our Lord!"[82]

In an instant the souls of redeemed humanity undergo a magnificent transformation! Each saint is sheathed with a new glorified body—the truest and purest representation of themselves—forever youthful and amazingly strong. A robe of righteousness then materializes around them: intricately woven out of heavenly materials. These robes seem sentient... at some level alive... crafted out of the most vibrant of white fibers which glow as brilliant as the sun. And each robe is similar in form to the others, yet as unique in style as the redeemed saint who wears it. Then a crown, made of a substance similar to precious metals forms on the head of each saint; beginning with an inscribed stone in its center, wrapping around to the back of the head.[83]

Christ steps forward and gives two objects to each saint, individually yet instantly. The first is a white stone approximately the size of the palm of each person's hand. The second is a smaller, uniquely shaped object.

"Inscribed upon this stone is your new name," Jesus informs each person. "On Earth, many called you names which did not suit who you were becoming. Those names brought you tremendous pain and confusion. Each name you internalized caused you to smother an aspect of the dignity, which our Heavenly Father invested in you, as an heir to his Kingdom. But here, the name on this stone is how I've always known you. It represents your true identity—who you truly are to me and within me." All of the saints look at their new name which is etched into the stone... their true name... and they rejoice![84]

Jesus then hands each saint the second object, which pulsates with immense power and glory. Once received, it bonds with them.

"This is the morning star," Jesus adds with a hint of mystery.[85]

"What do we do with this?" a saint inquires with great curiosity.

Jesus smiles deeply. "Just as on Earth, it is true here. There is beauty in the mysterious unfolding of an adventure."

"But, I have so many questions," a woman responds.

"We all do!" another adds.

Jesus laughs heartily. "And I have the answers you seek! All will be revealed in its proper order. For now, let us enter into the joy of our Father's Presence!"

Just then, the gates to the Kingdom appear. The saints are filled with wonder at the dazzling splendor of it all! Music, unlike any earthly ear has heard, saturates the atmosphere as the gates open. Immediately, wave after wave of God's love rolls over them as an ocean—saturating every ounce of their being! And a great crowd of heavenly citizens—those who had already come to glory in times past—stand in the distance cheering with innumerable angels at the homecoming of the saints. As the redeemed enter, many whisper with a newfound joy, "It's more beautiful than I ever imagined!"

"Lord!" another saint exclaims, "How did your single sacrifice for humanity accomplish all of this?"

"Come," Christ declares with a glimmer of victory in his eyes, "let me show you the power which resides in my blood."

And this... is just the beginning of the new things to come! ∎

ΑΩ

OUR RESURRECTED BODIES...

"Dear friends, now we are children of God, and what we will be has not yet been made known. But we know that when Christ appears, we shall be like him, for we shall see him as he is..."

"And we all, who with unveiled faces reflect the Lord's glory, are being transformed into his image with ever-increasing glory, which comes from the Lord, who is the Spirit." [86]

With the shout of the archangel, in a flash of brilliance we shall be changed from corruptible to incorruptible... from mortal to immortal... from flawed to perfection. Our souls will be given new resurrected bodies—like Christ's—which will NEVER decay! Weakness and frailty will be exchanged for strength and invulnerability. Limited reasoning will be exchanged for the capacity for near limitless understanding! LIFE in all its fullness will become the 'new normal' as our very existence will draw directly from the inexhaustible reserves of God himself!

Imagine having a physical body fashioned after that of Jesus. You can stand on the streets of gold in the New Jerusalem City or in a lush green field on the New Earth and choose whether to walk, run, fly or just "think" where you want to be and instantaneously be there! You can stand at the edge of the River of Life and choose to swim or walk the waves! You can look up into the sky and fly with the birds and soar through the cosmos with the angels!

You may ask, "Why do I believe this to be true?" Because our resurrected bodies will be like the resurrected body of Christ! Even *before* the resurrection he walked on water and did other amazing feats. After the resurrection, he teleported from place to place and flew into the sky! Oh, how our imaginations can barely comprehend all that will be possible for us to know and do![87]

"Eyes have not seen. Ears have not heard. Neither has it entered into the mind of them, what good things God has laid in store for them who love him. But, he has made them known through his Holy Spirit..."[88]

ΑΩ

A NEW CREATION...

One thing is sure... as fantastic as our earthly life is right now, our resurrected life will be infinitely better. Also, as awe-inspiring as our dreams and imaginations of that future can be, they pale in comparison to the glory and sheer excitement that awaits us! For the One who declared, "Old things are passed away. Behold! All things have been made new!" has planned a future for us that is unimaginable and has no semblance of anything boring![89]

Most people believe we go to heaven when we die and will live there forever. And many believe that life in heaven will consist of us living on clouds and playing harps as boredom eventually sets in, because all we will do is sing worship songs to God for all eternity. **But that is not the story God is telling!** Heaven, while immensely wonderful, is the staging area for God's next great creative act. For what God is about to do is beyond human imagination. But let's try to use our imaginations to visualize what God has *already* revealed to us in the Scriptures.

THE RENEWAL OF ALL THINGS...

*"Jesus said to them, 'Truly I tell you, **at the renewal of all things,** when the Son of Man sits on his glorious throne, you who have followed me will also sit on twelve thrones, judging the twelve tribes of Israel. And everyone who has left houses or brothers or sisters or father or mother or wife or children or fields for my sake will receive a hundred times as much and will inherit eternal life."* **- Matthew 19: 28-29**

It is the time of renewal... The universe ends in a clap! God folds it away—it having served its purpose to birth us into his Presence.[89.1] The volume complete, God places it in his vault of finished works and begins again with a new volume of the epic saga he has been telling across the ages. He is our consummate Creator who never sleeps. We, his newly redeemed humanity stand at the helm as witnesses. God opens his hand with a shout, and a **NEW UNIVERSE** springs forth across an empty multi-dimensional canvas. It is infinite in beauty and has complexity beyond the previous creation. Then God crafts a **NEW EARTH**... resplendent in unspeakable glory. **AND ALL THAT WAS TRAGICALLY LOST HAS NOW BEEN OVERWHELMINGLY RESTORED!**

This is the stuff of legends! Every hope of the human race... every longing that was ever good! Every fantasy story we love, where light ultimately triumphs over darkness and every enemy is vanquished. This unspeakable glory is the culmination of every account in human history where dictators have fallen and once oppressed citizens now rejoice in the streets!

This glory is hinted upon by your BEST days... It is felt, in part, every time you embrace someone you love, or hear a child's infectious laughter, or have your breath taken away by the stunning beauty of nature. It is tasted in small part, every time you eat your favorite food until you are thoroughly satisfied. It is even experienced on your WORST days. You know those moments when you feel like you can't take another step, but then an unexplainable grace shores up your soul. The joy of the new things God will do are all of these experiences rolled into one and multiplied by infinity!

Actually, the *reality* of Eternity is even greater than that! What God has planned for those who love him is beyond the ability of earthly languages to describe. It is as different an existence as our lives are different outside of our mother's womb! None of us remember what it was like during those first nine months. Chances are, in a similar fashion, the life we currently are living—at least all that is negative—will become a distant memory once we step into eternity and time gives way to forever!

Oh, to try to imagine this ultimate reality truly boggles the mind! But let us continue to do so. Can you see it? We Get It All! God gives us himself—first and foremost—an unhindered relationship overflowing with incomprehensible love, joy, peace and power! He gives us a vast new universe, with new physics, galaxies, and untold wonders free for us to explore! He gives us a new Earth, a place to live WITHOUT the faintest trace of corruption! He gives us a new city to live in; the intricacy and beauty of which will make our current best architectural efforts seem like kindergarten blocks. And God will make his actual dwelling WITH us... truly Heaven on Earth. Just look…

"I saw the Holy City, the new Jerusalem, coming down out of heaven from God, prepared as a bride beautifully dressed for her husband. And I heard a loud voice from the throne saying, "Look! God's dwelling place is now among the people, and he will dwell with them. They will be his people, and God himself will be with them and be their God" (Revelation 21: 2-3).

Read the rest of Revelation 21… The New Jerusalem city will be full of glory and light! It is made from the most precious materials in the universe and the purest of gold—so pure it is like clear glass. The colors bursting forth, radiating in every direction! It descends from heaven to earth. Its four walls form the shape of a cube with twelve gates for entrance. Three gates on the north. Three on the south. Three to the east. Three to the west. Can you imagine it? The breadth of the city is almost as large as the entire United States. Its height reaches high into Earth's orbit. Imagine entering at ground level and flying to its top in outer space! And we can't even begin to picture what our homes will be like!

"Then the angel showed me the river of the water of life, as clear as crystal, flowing from the throne of God and of the Lamb down the middle of the great street of the city. On each side of the river stood the tree of life, bearing twelve crops of fruit, yielding its fruit every month. And the leaves of the tree are for the healing of the nations." (Revelation 22: 1-2)

A pure river of living water, more majestic and robust than the Amazon and Nile rivers combined, flows from the city's center where God's Throne rests. And this river most likely stretches throughout the Earth. Trees of Life—the same as in the Garden of Eden—bank both sides of the river. In Eden, God had to separate fallen humanity from the tree of life in order to secure us for this very moment! Oh, to finally be able to eat of its fruit, uncorrupted, in full view with God's affirmation!

AΩ

A MATCH MADE IN HEAVEN... AND EARTH

It may be hard to envision (especially if you are a man), but Christ will declare his eternal love for us as a husband declares his love for his wife! In a very real sense, Christ *is* the Bridegroom and we—his redeemed humanity—*are* his bride. What this means is that God, who is the originator of marriage makes the ultimate declaration of his love, which goes *BEYOND* "Til death do we part" because he has conquered death and every other force of derailment!

We will fully receive his overwhelming love and love him in return. And we will forever be with the Lord. There will be no miscommunication, no irreconcilable differences, no abuse, no separation, no divorce! The fruit of the Holy Spirit will reign in our relationship with Christ for all eternity!

As a husband and wife are "two becoming one," so Christ and redeemed humanity are "many who become one." We are and will be "bone of Christ's bone, flesh of his flesh and spirit of his Spirit!" **The marriage of the Lamb and the Bride will finally come and nothing will stand between us and God—God and us!** [90]

And oh, the banquet feast which follows! This will be a time of exquisite delicacies human taste buds have yet to imagine, enjoyed in a most intimate fellowship. Imagine the types of stories and conversations we will have—not just with those we've known who have died in the LORD, *but with all the family of God*! I already have a growing list of saints I want to talk to on that day. Don't you? This type of fellowship is not fully possible in the here and now, yet it is one we are given glimpses of in our most soul-searching moments between two friends, two spouses, a parent and a child, and even strangers who have risked their lives for one another.

Think of those moments when you have connected with someone on the deepest level that exists beyond words...where there was no pretense and no shame. This heavenly fellowship which awaits us, is one where there are no contentions, no misunderstandings, no hatred, no jealousy, no gossip, no envy, no lying, and no cheating. A fellowship where love reigns supreme, joy overflows like a river, and genuine understanding abounds forever![91]

Everything we have ever sought for, fought for, and died for rests in this vision provided in the Holy Scriptures. It is all we instinctively knew in the back of our minds and in the deepest recesses of our hearts... that we had lost and longed to return to. God grants all of this to us—PERFECTED. There will be no more blemishes. There will be no deformity. There will be no more death. There will be no possibility of fallen nature. Evil in all of its forms will be erased from existence never to arise again.

Jesus, the last Adam restores what the first Adam relinquished: a full, unhindered relationship with the God of the universe. And as this all takes place, Jesus Christ—God the Son—will turn everything over to the Father and all will be completely right once more. **It is here, at this moment, that the deep, hidden, eternal plan which**

was held in the bosom of God alone will be fully revealed, and we will discover the "why" behind everything—behind Lucifer's rebellion, humanity's fall and God's redemption.[92]

AΩ

GOD'S CENTRAL PURPOSE

THIS is God's central revealed purpose. Through the crucifixion and resurrection of Jesus Christ, God reconciles humanity to himself, destroys the works of Satan, overcomes death, and completely restores his original intention of an intimate fellowship with his human image bearers. Both a newly restored universe and earth will be united with heaven, and this restoration will last forever! We will know our Creator for who he is as our work and worship unite!

Just think about the amazing discoveries and innovations humanity has been able to achieve thus far—*in our fallen and sinful state.* Imagine what we will be able to accomplish in a risen and perfected existence! Dare I say that we can't imagine it! The possibilities are too staggering! We will utilize our gifts and talents on a level unimagined as we work for God's pleasure. Yes, work **and** worship will be exciting and fulfilling! For we will worship God ***through*** working in his purpose for us.

This sounds fantastic and perhaps, to some of us, too good to be true. It may even seem downright inconceivable! But, this is the Grand Story given to us through the Bible. And it is the Story which makes the best sense out of the evidence creation provides. We are not cosmic accidents living only to vanish away into the darkness of an indifferent universe! We were created on purpose—for a purpose!

And what JESUS promises to those of us who follow him **can be trusted.** He declares, "I Am the Way, the Truth and the Life. No one comes to the Father but by me."[93] How wonderful to know God has made a way for us to know him! How amazing it is to realize that the All-Powerful One not only creates, but also transforms his creation. This is the Great Mystery that is playing out—scene by scene—before our very eyes!

CLOSING THOUGHTS ON THE GOSPEL OF JESUS CHRIST

Hopefully, now that you have read this grand narrative, you realize how central Jesus is to everything. The good news he brings rests solely on the reality of his pre-existence, his virgin birth, his death on the cross and his resurrection from the dead—never to die again! While God's purpose for us is resurrection through Christ, I want to try and shed a bit more light on the significance of resurrection by taking a closer look at the death of Jesus. Then, I will share some thoughts on what it means to fully receive this good news of resurrection into our own lives.

ΑΩ

In the garden of Gethsemane, Jesus was overwhelmed with sorrow as he contemplated his coming death. He was so overwhelmed that he cried out, "Abba Father. Everything is possible for you. Take this cup from me. Yet not what I will, but what you will." (Mark 14:36)

Most of us believe Jesus had a crisis between what he knew he had to do and what he wanted to do, because he did not want to die. After all, much of our time on earth is consumed with fear as we try to prevent our own physical death. But was the sorrow Jesus experienced due to his fear of physical death? Or was it something deeper?

After all, what is physical death to the One who is the "Resurrection and the Life?" What is bodily death to the One who repeatedly raised the dead with as much ease as getting out of bed after waking from sleep?

WAS IT PHYSICAL DEATH?

I submit to you that, although the suffering of his beating, flogging and crucifixion would be great, the primary concern of Jesus was *not* his physical death.

Here is what he clearly stated in John 10:18, "No one takes my life from me. I give it up willingly! I have the power to give it up and the power to receive it back again, just as my Father commanded me to do" (CEV). So, the death of the body was not his concern. However, **the death of the soul** was something he had never experienced before at all—from his eternal pre-existent state up to that very moment in the garden. Even though it had been predetermined before the earth was created that he would be the Lamb of God who would take away the sins of the world, he still had to walk it out in the "here and now."

There were two things Jesus was about to experience that gave him such pause, that when he prayed to his Father, blood vessels burst due to his mental agony and caused sweat—mixed with blood—to drip from his forehead. These two things were sin and death.

DOING WHAT NO ONE ELSE COULD DO

First, Jesus was literally going to become sin—the very thing which would separate him from his eternal fellowship with the Father and the Holy Spirit.

2 Corinthians 5:21 declares the agreement the Heavenly Father had with the Son and the Holy Spirit in order to secure salvation for those of us who would believe: "For he has made him to be sin for us, who knew no sin; that we might be made the righteousness of God in him."

As the second Person of the Divine Godhead, he had never known isolation before! But, on the cross, he was about to be plunged into the greatest isolation imaginable. All of this was about to happen because sin cannot be in God's direct Presence without being judged. Jesus was about to become the very thing which he hated... He would take on the sin–not of a single person–but of **all** the inhabitants of the entire world—past, present and future. And why would he do this? So we might take on *his* righteousness and be received as purified to our Heavenly Father.

Second, Jesus was about to experience—for every human—the death that is beyond death. The Bible calls this the second death in Revelation 2:11. It is an eternal oblivion where those who have rejected God in this earthly life, will suffer in torment forever.

The Bible declares in Hebrews 2:9 that Jesus tasted death for every person. Why? So, we would not have to taste it ourselves. Well, if it only referred to physical death, then once Jesus died on the cross and resurrected on the third day, no one should ever physically die again! As this is not the case, there must be a death beyond mere physical death.

Jesus himself declared in John 11:25, "I am the resurrection and the life. The one who believes in me will live, even though they die; and whoever lives by believing in me will never die. Do you believe this?" He is clearly speaking about two kinds of death... a death of the body and a death of the soul. And if we have to taste the second death ourselves, it will take all eternity to pay for our own sins. *(In other words, we would forever suffer for them.)*

THE NATURE OF SIN AND DEATH

"The depravity of man is at once the most empirically verifiable reality but at the same time the most intellectually resisted fact." - **Malcolm Muggeridge**

None of what has been said thus far makes sense if you minimize the corrupting effects and ravaging nature of sin. Neither does it make sense if you disregard God's right as the Creator of all things to bring judgment due to sinful rebellion. Sin is more than an error in our decision making, a mistake, or a disability. It is a cancer which lies at the core of who we are as a fallen humanity. And it knows only one purpose: to consume life in order to replicate death.

Sin stands at odds against a God who is as holy and pure as it is unholy and vile. The effects of sin is the ultimate pandemic which corrupts humanity and creation so thoroughly that there is no remedy for our predicament except the shed blood of Jesus. Sin cannot be washed away or legislated into submission by human laws. It is a supernatural occurrence with temporal and eternal consequences so devastating that Christ had to come to earth in the flesh to adequately eradicate it himself!

"Yet it was the LORD's will to crush him and cause him to suffer, and though the LORD makes his life an offering for sin, he will see his offspring and prolong his days, and the will of the LORD will prosper in his hand." (Isaiah 53:10)

In the Garden of Gethsemane great sorrow overtook Jesus because he knew the time of fulfillment had come. He was about to be separated from his Father. He was going to receive the full brunt of his Father's wrath—the rightful judgment of an infinite holy God on rebellious sin. Jesus would endure this punishment and torture not because he deserved it, but as an act of love towards his Father and towards humanity. This decisive act was already determined *(by the God of the universe who knows all things and all possibilities)* to be the **only** way to adequately and truly redeem a fallen humanity.

What has Christ redeemed us from? From the influence and consequences of an eternal state of destruction reserved for the devil and his angels. Jesus Christ, the eternal Son of God, was about to cross over the ultimate threshold of evil and allow sin and death to fully consume his being in order to destroy both forever. The staggering nature of the undertaking he was about to endure gave him pause. Yet, even in his distress, he was able to proclaim, "not my will, but your will be done."

FIX YOUR EYES ON JESUS

You may be wondering how he was able to endure the suffering and humiliation of the cross. Here is what Hebrews 12: 2 says: "Fixing our eyes on Jesus, the pioneer and perfecter of faith. For the joy set before him he endured the cross, scorning its shame, and sat down at the right hand of the throne of God."

Jesus endured the wrath of his Father, on our behalf, by focusing on the joyful results of his sacrifice: Salvation brought to us. Restoration from sin and death (in all of its forms) by resurrection. The dethroning of Satan and evil from the hearts of all who believe. Being reunited with his Father... forever taking his seat of authority at the right hand of the throne of God.

May you and I never fear physical death again. Christ's sacrifice on our behalf was (and continues to be) thorough and fully sufficient! In him, we no longer have to fear the second death either, because those who belong to Christ will never experience it. He has tasted death so we don't have to! And he has replaced the death and suffering which dwelled in our hearts, with raging torrents of life. What an amazing display of the unbridled love of our Lord and Savior!

For me, the following two Scripture verses highlight the significance of Christ's death and resurrection:

"...that God was reconciling the world to himself in Christ, not counting people's sins against them. And he has committed to us the message of reconciliation." (2 Corinthians 5:19)

"For if, while we were God's enemies, we were reconciled to him through the death of his Son, how much more, having been reconciled, shall we be saved through his life!" (Romans 5:10)

We have a Heavenly Father who loves us so much that he sent his Son to save us. And we worship Jesus, the Son, who loved his Father so completely, that he was obedient to the plan of salvation even to death.

AΩ

For the rest of this chapter, I want us to take a look at what it means to fully receive this beautiful and challenging message of salvation into our lives. Then we will close with considering how the resurrection of Jesus Christ changes everything!

AΩ

Again, Jesus Christ did for us, what we were incapable of doing for ourselves. We cannot add anything to his finished work. Salvation cannot be earned by trying to work for it. It is the grace of God which opens the door to us, and it is our faith which enables us to walk through the door God has provided. Through the shedding of his glorious blood, his death on the cross and his resurrection from the dead on the third day, Jesus has secured an eternal salvation for all who believe. It is eternal because he is eternal. And so, any good works we do are to be done out of gratitude and love for what Christ has already accomplished for us!

"I am the gate; whoever enters through me will be saved. They will come in and go out, and find pasture. The thief comes only to steal and kill and destroy; I have come that they may have life, and have it to the full." **-Jesus (John 10:9-10)**

"I am the way and the truth and the life. No one comes to the Father except through me." **-Jesus (John 14:6)**

In the Introduction, I asked the question, "What is Christ resurrecting us for?" I have sought to answer that question within the pages of this book. But the answer can be summed up in one sentence: **Jesus Christ is resurrecting us for himself and for his Father's eternal purpose.**

Jesus states it this way in John 14: 1-3, *"Don't let your hearts be troubled. Trust in God, and trust also in me. There is more than enough room in my Father's home. If this were not so, would I have told you that I am going to prepare a place for you? When everything is ready, I will come and get you, so that you will always be with me where I am."* (NLT)

Here is what Ephesians 2:6-7 says, *"And God raised us up with Christ and seated us with him in the heavenly realms in Christ Jesus, in order that in the coming ages he might show the incomparable riches of his grace, expressed in his kindness to us in Christ Jesus."* (NIV)

The Bible declares that Jesus gave himself for our sins, that he might deliver us from the evil of this world. The Bible also states that we are not made right in God's eyes by the work of the Law, but by placing our faith in Jesus Christ. If we could become righteous and acceptable before God on our own, by obeying the law (doing enough good works) then Jesus would not have had to die for us.[94]

Many of us may be living our lives based on a formula where we are trying to do enough good works to outweigh our bad deeds, in hopes of God receiving us into his presence. However, God has an entirely different system of measurement that he uses to determine our right standing before him: His Son Jesus. The Old Testament Law is meant to show us that we *can't* keep it. It is the mirror that is held before our faces so we can see ourselves as we truly are. It is meant to reveal the truth—that we are flawed individuals who are in need of a Savior. It is meant to lead us into the loving arms of God's grace.[95.1]

The question is, <u>will you accept God's assessment of the human heart?</u> That, apart from Jesus living in us, our heart is deceptively wicked.[95] That we are dead without Christ and the only remedy for our "heart disease" is for us to surrender our lives to Jesus so he can perform "heart surgery" within us in order to provide us with a new existence.[96]

Perhaps you are reading this and thinking, *Is it really this deep and serious? Does it really take all of this? Isn't it just enough to believe that God exists? I'm a good person. At least I am not as bad as someone else.*

"God didn't come to make bad people good. He came to make dead people live." **-Ravi Zacharias, Christian Apologist**

YOUR WORLDVIEW

Everything is dependent on what you think about the nature of reality. This is called a worldview: what you believe when you examine life. All of us view the world and generally come to one of two conclusions.

One: Believe there is nothing supernatural about the universe. The universe spontaneously created itself at random with no Intelligence at the helm. All of the precise physical laws that govern the universe happened by chance. All of the extremely simple and incredibly complex lifeforms on Earth got here by accident (or by aliens). All that exists is a physical dimension made up of matter and energy. There is no Moral Agency behind it all. There is no judgment for what we do here. There is no spirit and no soul. Evil is just a glitch in the matrix of our DNA programming. Life is just biological machines running until they break down beyond repair. And when we die... our lives end—in totality.

Two: Believe the universe sprang forth from the supernatural. A Creator brought the universe into existence and established the precise physical laws that govern its motion. Earth was designed to be inhabitable. All of the extremely simple and incredibly complex life on Earth was placed here on purpose *(but not by aliens)*. The universe consists of matter, energy, and spirit. There is a Moral Agency behind it all. Human life is more than just biology. And when our physical bodies die... the essence of who we are (our soul) lives on and will come before our Creator for judgment on how we lived.

WHAT DO YOU BELIEVE?

If you believe that everything comes down to random chance and there's nothing beyond the physical, then ultimately, nothing we do matters at all. We are here today, gone tomorrow, never to be seen again. If there's no Moral Agency in the universe, then the morality we use to judge between good and evil is just an illusion. We can live however we desire and do what we want with no fear of retribution beyond the physical consequences our societal laws demand.

However, if you believe there is a Moral Agency behind the creation and workings of the universe, then we are indeed held accountable for how we live. If one thing matters, then everything matters. And if there are moral laws and moral truths that we hold to be true, then there must be a Moral Lawgiver who provides the standard by which we make the distinctions between good and evil. And if there is a standard about what is good and evil, then that standard must be absolute, because something cannot be truly evil today and then good tomorrow *(or vice versa)*.

"Christianity, if false, is of no importance, and if true, is of INFINITE IMPORTANCE. The only thing it cannot be is moderately important."
-C.S. Lewis, British Novelist, Christian Apologist

If you and I are more than just biological machines, then the question becomes, *how* do we live? How do we discover the truth? How do we prepare for eternity, where we will find ourselves standing before this Moral Agent? And who is this Moral Agent?

Why is there something (the universe) rather than nothing? We are finite creations, who can examine things from "the inside out." We gain some general revelation about the makeup of the universe and conclude it is inextricably fine-tuned and very complex. It shows all the hints of being designed. And when we see things that have been designed, like a car, an airplane, a book, a building, a watch and a host of other things, we look for the intelligent designer who created them. Yet, why is it that when some see the universe, they readily assume that it happened by chance? Could it be, their own biases color the truth to make it unseen to their eyes—just like color filtering glasses kids sometimes play with?

According to the Bible, in Psalm 19:1, "The heavens declare God's glory." The evidence for God's existence is present for anyone who *wants* to see. But if the universe is too big for you to consider, then examine the evidence within your own body—which is a universe of a different sort. Dr. John Lennox, a Professor of Mathematics at the University of Oxford, puts it this way:

"We have only to see a few letters of the alphabet spelling our name in the sand to recognize at once the work of an intelligent agent. How much more likely then, is the existence of an intelligent Creator behind human DNA, the colossal biological database that contains no fewer than 3.5 billion letters—the longest 'word' yet discovered?"

The questions remain: If the universe was designed, then **WHO** is the Designer? **WHAT** were we designed for? And can we **KNOW** this Designer for ourselves? Here is what King David said in Psalms:

"What are humans that God is mindful of them? Why do you visit us? You have made us slightly lower than the angels. You have crowned us with glory and honor."[97]

The Bible gives the clearest answer to these questions. The Moral Agent Designer is the Being we call God. Through the Bible, he has revealed to us the names he calls himself.[98] And God has spoken (revealed) to us his plan from "the outside in." God has the clearest picture of everything, because of his infinite knowledge, wisdom, power and eternal vantage point. So, he reveals to us what we cannot see from our limited position in time and space. But to believe this is even possible and plausible, you must have a worldview, which *allows* for the supernatural to intervene in the realm of the natural!

Those who subscribe to the non-existence of God do not want to be held accountable for how they live. They see the same evidence as those who believe in God, yet they want to make their own way in life. They want to live by their own estimation of what is good and evil.

THE GOOD NEWS

So, what is the Good News? God does for us what we cannot do for ourselves. We are slaves to sin, doomed to perish if left to our own devices, but God was in Christ, reconciling the world back to himself.

This Good News declares that we are not accidents! We are not a result of random chance and unguided processes in an indifferent universe. We were created on purpose for a purpose! We were given gifts and talents for a purpose. *That purpose* is to bring glory, in this life and the next, to God who created us. Life continues after physical death and the quality of your afterlife—where you will spend eternity—depends on what you do with your life now.

The Good News reveals: Whoever you are, wherever you live, whatever the level of your social standing in life, God loves you and wants to restore his relationship with you through his Son, Jesus Christ.

The Good News declares: the evil you see in the world and the struggle you experience within yourself does not have to consume you. You can choose to repent of your sins and yield your life to Christ. To repent means to feel remorse for your wrongdoings, admit them, ask for forgiveness and turn away from those things you know do not please God.

The Good News reveals: God wants to be with you NOW and he wants you to be with him for all eternity. Now THAT is good news! You don't have to go through life feeling alone. He **is with** you! This is only possible by placing your trust and reliance in Jesus. This trust is two-fold. This first means believing in his sacrifice on the cross—that his blood which was shed washes away your sins. Second, it also means believing that his resurrection from the dead gives you the power to become a child of God. As God's child, eternal death no longer has a grip on you.

Jesus is more than a "good man" or a "good teacher." He is the Son of God. He is the Creator, Sustainer and Savior of the world. He is the Pioneer and Perfecter of your faith! He is the Son of Man of Daniel 7 who will judge us all. And he has a plan for your life that's bigger than you. If you are willing to yield yourself to him, then resurrection awaits!

DOES THIS CHANGE EVERYTHING?

Does Jesus being resurrected from the dead change everything? Not just for us in eternity, but also in our here-and-now? In many ways we are wedded to the world system in which we live. Our lives are lived as if the resurrection never happened. We live as if what we have now is all there is. We fashion our day-to-day reality around our jobs, careers, money, family, politics, social responsibility and entertainment. As a result, we can go days, weeks or months at a time without seriously considering Jesus and the overflowing outcomes of his resurrected life.

We don't allow God's truth about Jesus to inform us—at least nowhere near the level and intensity it should. But Christ (who is our example) reminds us in John 5:19, that **everything he did on earth, to impact the lives of others, came through his continual focus and reliance on God's kingdom.** In other words, _he was so heavenly minded that he was of the utmost earthly good!_ Jesus acted based on what he saw, heard, and knew to be true; even when _that Truth_ went against the reality he faced in his day-to-day experience. He constantly drew power and ability and guidance from his heavenly Father in order to be effective in our here-and-now.

Wherever you are right now, whatever you are doing or are about to do, the resurrection of Jesus Christ matters in all things: How we love. What we accept and what we refuse. What we pursue. How we do business. How we treat others. How we respond when others treat us with disrespect. Who we help and who we don't. How we relax and entertain ourselves. How we go to war. How we work for peace. What we dream about. What we fear and what we don't. How we live. How we die. The resurrection of Jesus matters to all of it.

The best thing we can do is to realize this truth, ask God to help us understand its significance, and begin to surrender our lives to it. The apostles of Jesus Christ were able to follow God's plan for their lives and boldly go where no one had gone before because they encountered the resurrected Christ. They were able to overcome their fears, cultural prejudices, personal biases, and the opposition they faced because the resurrection of Jesus mattered more than anything else.

They had opportunities to say that the resurrection of Jesus was all a lie. But they didn't! They were determined to put their lives on the line for God's glory and pay the ultimate price of martyrdom because the resurrection of their Lord and Savior was REAL to them! Whatever they faced... however their earthly life would come to an end... they knew that Christ was indeed "the Resurrection and the Life" and would raise them again at the Last Day! The pain and disappointment weren't worthy to be compared to the glory that would be revealed on that day![98.1]

Ask yourself:

What would my life look like if I lived as if the resurrection of Jesus matters in everything?

What will God accomplish <u>through</u> me with this kind of mindset?

How does the resurrection free me to be who God has created me to be?

How does the resurrection change the way I treat others?

Can I allow it to change how I respond when someone else is promoted instead of me?

Can I allow it to change how I respond to those who oppose me?

Can it affect how I treat those who are ostracized and marginalized by a life of poverty and sickness?

How does the resurrection empower me to take risks for God's kingdom?

THE PROMISE OF RESURRECTION

Does this mean you will never have another problem or won't face difficulties? Not at all. Resurrection means nothing can ultimately hold you down. It means God will bring you through every difficulty. God will be with you in the midst of each trial, working out his will in you and those around you.[99]

Resurrection also means that even in your losses—loss of dreams, hopes, ambitions, health and love—nothing is ever wasted. I know what you are thinking. I have thought it too. We have fought so hard to hold onto THIS world and the treasures we have amassed in it. But Jesus makes it abundantly clear that whatever we have to give up in this life, in order to follow him, will be restored! Some of that restoration will happen in this life... The bulk that's left, God will restore at the end of time to be fully enjoyed and experienced in the life to come.[100]

If you find your life *primarily* in *this* world, then these words may be a disappointment to you. Perhaps you are like the rich young ruler who *wanted* to follow Jesus, but couldn't part with his wealth and status to do so, because his identity was wrapped up in them.[101] C.S. Lewis, one of the greatest Christian thinkers of the 20th century puts it this way in The Four Loves:

"We know that every natural impulse, however innocent in itself, may stand between God and us and may so become an idol."

As an aside, God's love for us will always challenge those areas of our lives where our identity is tied more to them, than to him. *That* challenge ties *directly* into his promise to you and me: This promise of resurrection. This declaration that we are in this world, but not of the world; that we are made for another world—the fullness that is to come.[102]

C.S. Lewis, speaks to this issue as well:

"If I find in myself desires which nothing in this world can satisfy, the only logical explanation is that I was made for another world."

The question is, *Why does God promise us resurrection?* First, he promises this to us because it's *TRUE*. Second, he promises resurrection to us so we can be **freed from the pull of the fallen world system** we encounter each day, in order to be free *to walk unhindered with Christ.*

A CRISIS OF TWO EARTHS

In Matthew 6:24, Jesus tells us we cannot serve two masters because our devotion will be divided. We won't be able to be "all in" to one because of the influence of the other. The two masters he refers to are God and mammon (money, status, or anything else we place in front of God). We have to make a conscious decision. The difficulty lies in the fact that for most of our lives, the fallen world system *we live in* has told us to "choose mammon" which basically means to choose self over all else.

We have a crisis on our hands.

Our current earth, with its fallen system, loudly declares that the pursuit of self, family and government are to be our <u>highest</u> aims in life—even if it means demoralizing others in order to do so. But there is a *new earth* on the horizon. *That* earth is ruled by a *better* Kingdom—where humanity's highest aim is to know God and to glorify him through every gift and talent we have been given. The pursuit of self is *not* the primary focus in *that* world. Rather, as we fall ever-deeper in love with God, we become increasingly like who he has created us to be! And we don't have to wait until that new earth *fully* arrives before we can start living in it!

<u>So, the question is:</u> *WHICH EARTH WILL YOU LIVE FOR?* Will you fight to hold onto this present, old world that is passing away? Or will you live for the *new earth* that has already begun to arrive in the hearts of everyone who *truly* believes?

If you believe that the resurrection of Jesus Christ changes everything, then these questions are of paramount importance! They point to a truth for every Christ-follower: <u>though you are **in** this world, you are no longer **of** this world.</u> In other words, you are no longer to live by the mandate of this present fallen system, but rather by the mandate of our living Christ. The pursuit of self, family and government, as your **highest** aim in life is not compatible with where Christ wants to take you. At any time he may require you to relinquish all three in order for his eternal plan for you to be accomplished.

"Whoever wants to be my disciple must deny themselves and take up their cross daily and follow me." - Jesus (Luke 9:23)

"What good is it for someone to gain the whole world, yet forfeit their soul?" -Jesus (Mark 8:36)

If you are able to receive Christ's promise of resurrection, then an adventure beyond your comprehension awaits! You will begin to discover God's truth and accomplish the works he prepared for you to do before the foundations of the world.[103]

Oh, how wonderful it is to live out the very reason for your creation… to live for God's glory, purpose and pleasure! It is a place of fulfillment, where life will never be the same. And even with the battles you will encounter; even with the ones you may lose… you *will* ultimately be victorious. Why? Because Jesus is ultimately the Victor! So, in him, that makes you more than a conqueror![103.1]

How amazing it is to know that our experience here on earth is not the end. We are in fact, characters in the wonderful saga God, the Grand Author, has been telling throughout all eternity! And for those of us who truly believe… *that* story will **never** end![104]

Philippians 3:20-21 states it this way:

"20But our citizenship is in heaven. And we eagerly await a Savior from there, the Lord Jesus Christ, 21who, by the power that enables him to bring everything under his control, will transform our lowly bodies so that they will be like his glorious body."

As stated at the beginning of this book, everything about God's purpose for us and our deep longings hinges on the resurrection of Jesus Christ. Read the following passage from 1 Corinthians 15 and see how, through Christ, we will be raised to life as well!

42 In the same way, our earthly bodies which die and decay are different from the bodies we shall have when we come back to life again, for they will never die.

43 The bodies we have now embarrass us, for they become sick and die; but they will be full of glory when we come back to life again. Yes, they are weak, dying bodies now, but when we live again they will be full of strength.

44 They are just human bodies at death, but when they come back to life they will be superhuman bodies. For just as there are natural, human bodies, there are also supernatural, spiritual bodies.

45 The Scriptures tell us that the first man, Adam, was given a natural, human body but Christ is more than that, for he was life-giving Spirit.

46 First, then, we have these human bodies, and later on God gives us spiritual, heavenly bodies.

47 Adam was made from the dust of the earth, but Christ came from heaven above.

48 Every human being has a body just like Adam's, made of dust, but all who become Christ's will have the same kind of body as his—a body from heaven.

49 Just as each of us now has a body like Adam's, so we shall someday have a body like Christ's.

50 I tell you this, my brothers: an earthly body made of flesh and blood cannot get into God's Kingdom. These perishable bodies of ours are not the right kind to live forever.

51 But I am telling you this strange and wonderful secret: we shall not all die, but we shall all be given new bodies!

52 It will all happen in a moment, in the twinkling of an eye, when the last trumpet is blown. For there will be a trumpet blast from the sky, and all the Christians who have died will suddenly become alive, with new bodies that will never, never die; and then we who are still alive shall suddenly have new bodies too.

53 *For our earthly bodies, the ones we have now that can die, must be transformed into heavenly bodies that cannot perish but will live forever.*

54 *When this happens, then at last this Scripture will come true—"Death is swallowed up in victory."*

55-56 *O death, where then your victory? Where then your sting? For sin— the sting that causes death—will all be gone; and the law, which reveals our sins, will no longer be our judge.*

57 *How we thank God for all of this! It is he who makes us victorious through Jesus Christ our Lord!*

58 *So, my dear brothers, since future victory is sure, be strong and steady, always abounding in the Lord's work, for you know that nothing you do for the Lord is ever wasted as it would be if there were no resurrection.* (1 Corinthians 15:42-58, TLB)

<u>Here are two passages from the book of Hebrews:</u>

"Just as people are destined to die once, and after that to face judgment. so Christ was sacrificed once to take away the sins of many; and he will appear a second time, not to bear sin, but to bring salvation to those who are waiting for him." (Hebrews 9: 27-28)

"If they had been thinking of the country they had left, they would have had opportunity to return. Instead, they were longing for a better country—a heavenly one. Therefore God is not ashamed to be called their God, for he has prepared a city for them." (Hebrews 11:15-16)

ΑΩ

The Bible is very clear about the fantastic nature of reality and what God is doing in creation. And this book that you hold in your hands— RESURRECTION: The Big Picture of God's Purpose and Your Destiny—is like reading an abridged version of the Bible. Perhaps, it is even more like a sort of CliffsNotes. And like CliffsNotes, Resurrection should be read in conjunction with the Bible, not instead of the Bible. So, don't you want to find your place within the larger story of God's Word? Don't you want to see what God has promised you now and in the future to come? Don't you want to know how the story ends? Don't you want to read the prelude to the **NEW** story that begins after this one?" Read through the pages of Scripture and believe!

The resurrection of Jesus Christ changes everything!

EPILOGUE:

Thoughts on Satan's Great Deception

"There are two equal and opposite errors into which our race can fall about the devils. One is to disbelieve in their existence. The other is to believe and to feel an excessive and unhealthy interest in them. They themselves are equally pleased with both errors." **-C. S. Lewis, The Screwtape Letters**

Ever since the Fall in the garden of Eden—when Satan usurped humanity's authority and introduced sin into the world[105]—he has been fiendishly working to create a society which goes completely against the flow of God's Kingdom. This is why when Jesus came to earth, he was not readily received, but rather rejected. In a very tragic sense, the rightful ruler is not welcome in the world *he* created.[106]

Satan, as the god of this world and the prince of the air,[107] has used every resource at his disposal to create a counter narrative among humanity. It comes in three parts. Each aspect is efficient in its own right.

To the chosen few, this former "angel of light"[108] has revealed himself and aspects of his agenda. And they follow him tooth-and-nail in a deliberate attempt to refashion the world after his image.

To others, he imparts dreams of pantheons: idols created in their likeness. Those who fall by this wayside worship nature, inanimate objects, people they've idolized, and even demons rather than the Creator. [109]

However, to the minds of the masses, Satan has introduced the following propaganda in his bid for complete domination:

Humanity came to exist by chance. By the cosmic rolling of the dice we have evolved from single celled organisms, and fish, and monkeys. There is no God—no Intelligent Designer behind the scenes of the universe holding all things together. And if God does not exist, then neither can the devil. Both are mere fantasy dancing within the realm of our human imaginations. There is no war raging for our individual and collective souls.[110]

This lie grants him tremendous freedom to come and go as he pleases. With it he deceives and devours unsuspecting souls.[111] And so, he makes humans, the world over, believe that they were not created in God's image and likeness. This leads them to believe that there is nothing inherently special about their place in the universe at all.

He works so hard to conceal the truth, often in plain sight. You see Satan blinds us to the light of truth:[112]

Humanity didn't come into existence by chance. We did not accidentally form by the random collision of molecules and amino acids. The earth was, in fact, created to be inhabited. Humans were created in God's image to know him and to rule the earth by his leading. Great focus is placed on us, even though we are mere specks in the grand scale of the universe.[113]

A great war has indeed been raging between God and Satan for the sake of our souls. For God desires to give us dominion over his creation of both earth and skies. Yes, the universe is to be ours in the end as we reign with Christ. All of it given in a grand gesture of God's infinite love for his Son, through whom we have been redeemed. And this gesture... this eternal gift... we will unwrap and enjoy forever.[114]

It is hard for us to picture *"forever"* from this particular vantage point of time and space. And that is **precisely** what the devil is counting on! His whispers come often enough, misleading us to believe:

Forever is just an abstract conundrum wrapped up in a mystery chased by fools! **Here** *is where it's at! The temporal, what you can see, taste, touch, hear and smell is what truly matters! Do what you feel. Create your own meaning. The only absolutes are what you make! Eat. Drink. Be merry! You only live once—for tomorrow you die! And then... nothing. Just as you were nothing before you were born, you return to nothing when you die... just the cold oblivion of space, empty and void, with but specks of sparkles in between. There is no spiritual afterlife. There is no savior. There is no judgment. There is no resurrection.*[115]

But this is the great deception. And it **masquerades** as the truth.

APPENDIX
—

The first half of this book contains the Grand Story of Resurrection which God reveals in the Bible. This Appendix section contains additional information to help you grow in your walk with Christ.
—

CONTENTS:

*Scriptural References

*Study Guide

*How to Study the Bible

*Definition of Terms

*Articles of Faith

*20 Old Testament Prophecies About Jesus Christ

*7 Spiritual Disciplines

*The Mark of the Beast

*The Rapture

*Your Kingdom Come!

*Why Did Jesus Come?

*An Invitation to the Seeker

*An Invitation to the Christian

RESURRECTION STORY
Scriptural References

[1] John 11:25-26

[2] Colossians 1:16-17

[3] John 1:10-14; Isaiah 9:6

[4] 2 Corinthians 5:19

[5] 1 John 3:8; John 14:23; 1 Peter 1:3-4

[6] James 4:1

[7] Genesis 1:26; Genesis 3; Revelation 12:9

[8] Isaiah 45:18

[9] 2 Corinthians 5:17

[10] John 5:39

[11] John 19; Matthew 27; Mark 15; Luke 23

[12] Colossians 1:15-18; Hebrews 1:3; John 1:1-4; John 10:17-18

[13] John 3:16-18; Romans 3: 9-20, 23

[14] Genesis 1-3

[14.1] Job 38:1-7

[14.2] Isaiah 14:12-15; Ezekiel 28:12-19; Revelation 12:3-9

[15] Ezekiel 28:13-17; Revelation 12:7-9; Luke 10:18; John 8:44

[16] Genesis 3

[17] Psalm 51:5; Psalm 139:14

[18] Isaiah 64:6

[19] Romans 3:9-20; Exodus 33:18-23; Deuteronomy 4:23-24; Isaiah 6:1-7; Isaiah 59; Hebrews 12:29

[20] Genesis 6

[21] Genesis 12:1-3; Matthew 1:1-17; Luke 3:23-38; John 1:1-14

[22] Hebrews 10:5

[23] Isaiah 55:8-11

[24] Philippians 2:6-8

[25] John 1:29; Romans 8:32; 1 John 4:9-10; Isaiah 9:6-7

[26] John 3:1-3

[27] Hebrews 4:12; 1 Thessalonians 5:23; Ephesians 2:1-10; Genesis 2:17

[28] John 1:12-13; Ephesians 1:13-14; John 14:16; Romans 8:9, 29;
1 Corinthians 6:19-20; 1 Corinthians 12:13; John 3:6-8

[29] John 1:12-13

[30] John 3:3-8

[31] Isaiah 50:6; Isaiah 53:2-3; Matthew 26:27-29; Matthew 26:67;
Matthew 27:29-30; Luke 22:64; Hebrews 9:22

[32] Matthew 26:53-54

[32.1] Isaiah 53

[33] John 8:44; Revelation 12:9-11

[34] John 19:26; Matthew 26:53; 2 Kings 19:32-36

[35] Matthew 4:1-11

[36] Matthew 26:36-46; Mark 14:32-42; Luke 22:39-46

[37] Romans 8:17-18; Hebrews 12:1-3; John 3:16-18

[38] Matthew 21:37-39

[39] Luke 23:26-43

[40] Matthew 27:46; Psalm 22:1-2; Mark 15:34; 2 Corinthians 5:21

[41] Matthew 27:50-53

[42] Romans 5:6-11; Romans 1:18; Romans 3:23; 1 John 4:10; 1 John 2:2

[43] 2 Peter 3:9; 2 Corinthians 5:21

[44] Luke 22:20; Matthew 26:28; 1 Corinthians 11:25; Mark 14:24;
John 10:9-16; Matthew 12: 38-40; Romans 10:7; Ephesians 4:7-10

[45] Revelation 20:14-15; Matthew 25:41

[46] Luke 8:26-39; Mark 5:1-20; Ephesians 4:9; 1 Peter 5:8; 2 Peter 2:4;
Jude 1:6; Job 1:6-7

[47] Matthew 16:21; 20:18-19; John 2:19; 5:26; 10:17-18

[48] Matthew 27:57-66

[48.1] Luke 16: 19-31

[49] 1 Corinthians 15:53-57

[49.1] 1 Peter 3:18-19

[50] Acts 2:24; Hebrews 2:14

[51] John 6:44; 12:24; Colossians 1:15-19; Romans 8:29; 1 Corinthians
15: 28, 42-58; 2 Corinthians 5:19; 1 John 3:1-3

[52] Psalm 139:12

[53] John 14:12; Revelation 7:9; Matthew 28:18

[54] Mathew 28:1-10; Mark 16:1-11; Luke 24:1-12; John 20:1-18

[55] Psalm 19:1-6; Ephesians 4:10

[56] Revelation 4:8; (Genesis 1:26; Matthew 3:16-17; John 1:2) -
Evidence for the Trinity

[57] Isaiah 6:1-3; Revelation 4:9-11

[58] Hebrews 8:5; Hebrews 9:12-15; Hebrews 10:1-10

[59] John 20:19-23

[60] Mark 16:12-13; Luke 24:13-35

[61] Luke 24:36-49; John 20:19-23

[62] John 20:24-29

[63] John 20:30-31

[64] Acts 1:1-11; Matthew 28:16-20; John 14:1-3

[65] Acts 2:1-4; Exodus 3:1-5

[66] Luke 17:21

[67] Acts 2:40-47

[68] Isaiah 9:2; Matthew 4:16; Ephesians 5:8; 1 Peter 2:9

[69] Romans 8:16-18; Acts 20:32; Galatians 3:29; Ephesians 3:6;
Titus 3:7; Ephesians 1:3-14; Romans 8:28-30; Hebrews 2:10-11

[70] Matthew 24:3-14; 2 Thessalonians 2:1-3; 1 Timothy 4:1

[71] 2 Thessalonians 2:1-12; Daniel 7:25; Revelation 13:1-18;
1 John 2:18; 1 John 2:22; Daniel 7; Matthew 24:15-28;
Mark 13:22; Daniel 8:9-12; Daniel 11:36-45; Revelation 17:7-15;
Daniel 9:20-27; Revelation 12:5-6; Revelation 6:1-17;
Revelation 8; 9; 10; 11; 14:9-10; 16; 17; 18; 19

[72] Hebrews 9:27; Acts 17:31; John 5:21-30

[73] Revelation 20:1-5; Revelation 1:7; John 14:6

[74] James 2:19

[75] Ephesians 1:5; John 1:12; Galatians 4:4-5; Colossians 1:15;
Hebrews 2:10, 13

[76] Matthew 23:37; Mark 8:36; Matthew 16:26; Luke 9:25; Matthew 10:33

[77] Ephesians 2:8-9; Romans 3:23; 6:23

[78] John 3:16-21, 36; Colossians 2:13-15; 1 Thessalonians 1:9-10;
Philippians 3:18-19

[79] Matthew 12:35-37; John 5:21-30; Romans 2:1-16; Galatians 5:19-21; 2 Corinthians 5:9-11

[80] Revelation 20:10-15; Matthew 10:28; Daniel 7:7-27

[81] 1 Corinthians 3:11-15

[82] Ephesians 2:1-10; 2 Timothy 1:9; Titus 3:5; Matthew 25:21; 2 Corinthians 12:9; 2 Peter 1:1-11

[83] 1 Corinthians 9:24-25; 1 Peter 1:3-5; 2 Timothy 4:8; Philippians 3:20; 1 Peter 5:4; Revelation 7:9-10, 13-14; Colossians 3:12; Revelation 6:11

[84] Revelation 2:17

[85] Revelation 2:28

[86] 1 John 3:2, 2 Corinthians 3:18

[87] 1 Corinthians 15:35-58; Philippians 3:20-21; 1 Thess 4:13-18

[88] 1 Corinthians 2:9-10

[89] Matthew 19: 27-30; John 6:35-40; Revelation 21:5

[89.1] Hebrews 1:10-12; 2 Peter 3:7-13

[90] Matthew 25:1-13; Ephesians 5:22-32; Revelation 19:1-9

[91] Revelation 21:1-21; Revelation 22:1-5; Revelation 19:6-9

[92] 1 Corinthians 15:20-28, 45; Philippians 3:20-21; Philippians 2:9-11; Ephesians 3:8-12; Revelation 14:6-7

[93] John 14:6; Matthew 25:14-30

[94] Galatians 2:16, 21

[95] Jeremiah 17:9-10

[95.1] Galatians 3:21-24

[96] Ezekiel 36:25-27; Ephesians 2:1-10

[97] Psalm 8:4

[98] Exodus 3:13-15; John 5:14-20; John 8:48-58; Acts 4:8-12

[98.1] John 6:37-40; Romans 8:17-23

[99] John 16: 33; Romans 8:28-39

[100] Matthew 6:19-21; Matthew 19: 28-29; Mark 10: 29-30

[101] Matthew 19: 16-22; Mark 10:17-27; Luke 18:18-30;
    1 John 2:16-17

[102] Ecclesiastes 3:11; John 17:14-26; 2 Peter 1:1-11

[103] Ephesians 2:10; Philippians 1:6

[103.1] Romans 8:28, 31-39; John 16:33; Romans 14:7-9; Hebrews 12:2

[104] Ephesians 2:8-10; Psalm 139:13, 16; 1 Corinthians 2:9;
    Revelation 4:11; Revelation 21 & 22

[105] Genesis 3:1-15

[106] John 1:10-11

[107] 2 Corinthians 4:4; Ephesians 2:2

[108] 2 Corinthians 11:14-15

[109] Exodus 20: 3-6; Leviticus 19:4; Psalm 135:15-18; Isaiah 44: 9-20;
    Isaiah 45:10; Jonah 2:8; Galatians 4:8; Revelation 9: 20

[110] Psalm 14:1; Matthew 13:18-19; Mark 4:1-25; Luke 8:11-12;
    Ephesians 4:18; 6:10-18; 2 Corinthians 4:4; Colossians 1:16-18

[111] Job 1:6-12; John 10:10; 1 Peter 5:8-9; Revelation 20:1-3

[112] 2 Corinthians 4:4; Ephesians 2:2

[113] Psalm 8:1-9; Isaiah 45:18

[114] Revelation 21 & 22

[115] 2 Corinthians 4:17-18; Hebrews 9:27

RESURRECTION STUDY GUIDE

Congratulations! If you are reading these words, then you have finished reading about the BIG Picture of God's Purpose and Your Destiny! Perhaps you already knew the Grand Story God is telling us through the Bible. Maybe you only knew bits and pieces, or this is the first time you have heard it. Either way, you probably have questions about the Story.

This study guide has questions, quotes, Scriptures and insights which are based on key aspects of each section of the Grand Story. My hope is that this study guide will help you dive deeper into God's Word so you may *discover and know what God's plan and purpose is for your life (Romans 12:2).*

While you can go through this guide by yourself, it will be even more impactful if you do so with others. Don't short-circuit the process by skipping questions. Really take the time to wrestle with your answers, read the additional Scriptures and research the insights presented here. Your eternal destiny depends on it. May your journey continue. Enjoy!

INTRODUCTION:

1) What do you think of C.S. Lewis' quote below? Have you seen evidence of this insatiable desire in your own life or in others? Does Jesus provide us with a remedy for our dilemma?

"If we find ourselves with a desire which nothing in this world can satisfy, the most probable explanation is that we were made for another world."

2) Most people don't want to die. In fact, many fear death. (Refer to Hebrews 2:14-15). Why do you think people fear death? Do you fear death? Why or why not?

3) The quest for immortality lies at the heart of Transhumanism, (which I mentioned in the Introduction). It is defined as: *"the belief or theory that the human race can evolve beyond its current physical and mental limitations especially by means of science and technology."* At the center of this quest is the fear of death and the desire to become gods. Many of the great thinkers of our day, who are at the forefront of this movement which is reshaping the world culture and capturing the imaginations of this generation, are atheists/naturalists who deny God's claim on humanity.

Dr. John Lennox, a prominent scientist who is a Christian, has observed that people are trying to use science and technology to do what Jesus has already done. Here are several statements he shared during the talk: *Should We Fear Artificial Intelligence? (Available on Youtube.)*

"We have come to a very important moment where we can see in our culture ideas that are parodies of what we've already got in the Bible, which gives us a remarkable opportunity to speak into what's going on."

"The ultimate affirmation of humanity 1.0 [our current state] is that God became one... 'The Word became flesh and dwelt among us...' and the result of the incarnation, the death and resurrection of Jesus... that instead of speculative hope that one day we can upload the content of our brains [into computers] or we can be bio-engineered to live forever, we have a sure and certain hope based on the true Homo Deus... Jesus has already given us phase one of a divine upgrade! 'That to as many as received him, to them he gave the right to become children of God.' And phase 2 is spectacular! Because it is a transformation. It is not bio-engineering. We can lift up our heads in confidence because this is what it is... 'for the trump will sound and the dead will be raised imperishable and we shall be changed... this mortal must put on immortality.' That is the future of the Christian believer. And it is light years more credible and better than anything speculative that artificial intelligence has to offer." (Refer to John 1:12-14 and 1 Corinthians 15:50-58)

4) Where does our longing for eternal life come from? What does Ecclesiastes 3:11 say about the matter?

5) Utopia is defined as: *"An ideal place or state. Any visionary system of political and social perfection."* What is your idea of utopia? According to

the Bible, what vision of utopia does God have in mind for humanity? When will *that* utopia come? How can we experience aspects of it *now*, while we eagerly wait for its fullness to arrive? Why is it that humanity's attempts at utopia have failed and continue to do so?

6) A linchpin is defined as: *"something that holds various elements of a complicated structure together."* What are your thoughts on I Corinthians 15:16-26? How is this the linchpin of Christianity?

7) Scientists discovered that the visible part of the universe only accounts for about 5% of the universe's total volume. They do not know what makes up the 95% that is invisible. Whatever it is, it seems to be integral to the formation and function of the universe. Interestingly, the Bible declares that **Christ holds the universe together by his own power and that the visible was made from the invisible** (Colossians 1:15-17/ Hebrews 1:2-3/ Hebrews 11:3). This declaration, *which sounds very similar to scientific discovery,* was made almost 2000 years ago! Here's how Dr. John Lennox puts it:

"The primary reality of the universe is not mass and energy at all... it is Spirit. Mass and energy is a derivative."

What are your thoughts on this?

8) Do you believe we are born into a world at war? In what ways do you see this played out on a personal, societal, international and spiritual level? What does this seem to indicate about the nature of reality? Is there an unseen evil at work? How does God want us to wage warfare at each level? What tools does he provide for us to fight with? (Refer to: Matthew 5:44; Proverbs 4:23; 2 Corinthians 10:4-5; Ephesians 6:10-18; 2 Timothy 1:7 to get you started).

9) The Greek word for Resurrection is Anastasis. How does its definition as listed in the Introduction section of this book, bring hope for your future and your today?

10a) Give your thoughts on the following quote:

"Resurrection is not only restoring what was lost—it is also bestowing upon

us what we never had."

10b) We often use our imagination to envision our pain, hurt and worst-case-scenarios. But God has given us our imagination for a greater purpose. Take some time to imagine God healing and restoring what you have lost in life. Then imagine Christ bestowing upon you something you have never had... himself. (Refer to Colossians 1:10-12; 1 Peter 1:3-9).

PART 1: ORIGINS

1) The Bible paints a vivid picture of our reality being infinitely more amazing than we can imagine! It is supernatural in nature and filled with unseen celestial beings. We are not alone in the universe. There is one Supreme Being who rules it all. Yet, secular society peddles the Theory of Evolution as fact: that humanity is a product of random cosmic chance. That we evolved from single cell organisms over billions of years.

Although the educational and scientific community are proponents of the Theory of Evolution, there are many credible educators and scientists who look at the same evidence provided in creation and conclude: the universe did not get here by accident. Rather, it was created by a Supreme Intelligent Designer. How does what we believe about our origins and the nature of reality affect how we view others and live our own lives?

2) The Theory of Evolution leaves no room for Adam and Eve (humanity's first parents), Lucifer (who is the literal embodiment of all evil), the fall of humanity and the resulting sin introduced into the world. Without these key historical facts revealed to us in the Bible, how do we account for evil in the world and our fallen sinful condition? Here are two quotes by Malcolm Muggeridge which sum up our predicament:

"The depravity of man is at once the most empirically verifiable reality but at the same time the most intellectually resisted fact."

"One of the peculiar sins of the twentieth century which we've developed to a very high level is the sin of credulity. It has been said that when human beings stop believing in God they believe in nothing. The truth is much worse: they believe in anything."

3) Is it possible that the Theory of Evolution was created *(or at least supported)* in an effort to push God out of public thought in society?

4) Why was eating from the Tree of the Knowledge of Good and Evil so devastating? What ways do we see the consequences playing out in our world each day?

5) Notice that the tree is not called "the Knowledge of Evil," but of "Good and Evil." What's the significance of this? How does this fact impact our decision making? What does it indicate about our independence from God? What Scriptures can you find which support how God wants us to make our decisions?

6) According to the Bible, the origin of the universe (as well as us) is both physical and spiritual. What do you think this means?

7) After Adam and Eve sinned, why did God kick them out of the Garden of Eden? Was this a harsh punishment or something else entirely?

8) According to Part 1, humanity is caught in the middle of a war between Satan and God. What schemes does Satan use against us?

9) Did Adam and Eve have to sin? Was the prophecy of Christ coming to liberate the human race from the devil's tyranny an after-thought?

10) Why is it crucial for each person to be born again? Based on what you have read in this book, why is "being a good person" not enough?

11) What is the significance of God overshadowing Mary with his Holy Spirit in order for Jesus to be born without an earthly father? What does it reveal about the blood of Jesus?

PART 2: JESUS FIGHTS FOR US!

1) Do you know Jesus fought for you on the cross and continues to fight for you (from heaven) every day of your life? List at least 5 Scriptures which reveal how Jesus does this? (I'll give you one: John chapter 17).

2) What do you think 2 Corinthians 5:19 means when it says: "For God was in Christ, reconciling the world to himself, no longer counting

people's sins against them. And he gave us this wonderful message of reconciliation." (New Living Translation)

3) The Cat-o-nine tails was no ordinary whip. What kind of damage did it do to Jesus during his flogging? Remember, this was before he had to carry his 100-300 pound cross at least 2000 feet to where he would be crucified.

4) John the Baptist gave Jesus this title in John 1:29: "...the Lamb of God, who takes away the sin of the world!" How does Jesus being "the Lamb of God" relate to the Passover in Exodus chapter 11 to chapter 12:30?

5) What kept Jesus on the cross? Was it the nails in his hands and feet? Or something more?

6) Why did Jesus die for us? What does his death accomplish for us?

7) When Jesus died, his followers were devastated, his enemies were elated and Satan thought he had triumphed! But what looked like failure was actually a part of God's plan from the very beginning. How does reading about Jesus' death and resurrection from the physical and spiritual perspectives shed light on how God operates "behind the scenes" in our own lives?

8) Read 1 Corinthians 2:6-8. What can you learn about God's eternal purpose for our salvation? What do you discover about the secret nature of God's plan? What does this indicate about the knowledge base of Satan?

9) The Bible declares that the last enemy of God to be destroyed is Death (1 Corinthians 15:26). Once this happens, what will be left?

10) Read Matthew 26:28 and Hebrews 9:22. What do these reveal about the nature of the blood of Jesus and humanity's need for it?

PART 3: RESURRECTION!

1) The Bible declares that Jesus is the Firstborn among many brothers and sisters (Romans 8:29). It also declares in the same verse that God the Father is in the process of conforming us into the image of His Son. In light of this truth, what does Jesus' resurrection mean for us who believe,

trust and rely on him?

2) The Bible declares that when followers of Christ are resurrected, we will have new bodies like Christ's body (Philippians 3:21; 1 John 3:2). What exploits did Jesus do before and after his resurrection? What does this mean for us?

3) Many call the disciple Thomas, "Doubting Thomas" because he did not believe the testimony of the other disciples when they said they saw Jesus alive after his death. We don't know why he wasn't with the group when Jesus appeared to them. But his refusal to believe, ultimately speaks to his desire to have the same experience they had. However, what else does his doubt reveal? And how does Jesus confront Thomas about it several days later when he appears to the group again—this time Thomas being present? In what ways do we doubt God's ability to operate in our lives to do the impossible?

4) Why did Jesus spend 40 days with his disciples and other believers after his resurrection, but before his ascension? What would happen if you spent 40 days seeking Jesus' face by reading through the gospels? *(Read my companion book, The Resurrection Life, and find out.)*

5) What happened when Jesus encountered two of his disciples on the road to Emmaus after his resurrection? (Refer to Luke 24: 13-35)

6) What Prime Directive (Great Commission) did Jesus give to his disciples before returning to heaven? If you are a Christian, do you realize that your salvation is a direct result of the apostles' obedience to Christ almost 2000 years ago? You did not get saved in isolation. In fact, Jesus prayed specifically for you (and every believer) in John chapter 17.

7) What does it mean to you to know that Jesus has paid the debt for your sin and provides you with an eternal home with him? Do you realize that the corruption of sin is so grievous that if you had to pay the debt-penalty yourself it would take all eternity?

8) Why is it important for us to remember what the two angels said after Jesus left earth for heaven? Let's take a look at their words...

"Men of Galilee, why do you stand here gazing up to the sky? This same Jesus you just saw ascend into the clouds will return in like manner" (Acts 1:11).

How do their words keep us from being deceived by false prophets and messiahs?

PART 4: THE PROMISE FULFILLED

1) Read Acts 1:1-8. What promise did Jesus tell his disciples to wait for, before they were to begin carrying out the Great Commission? Why did Jesus say it was necessary?

2) This same promise is made to us as well. Why do we need to receive God's Holy Spirit in our own lives?

3) Read the following: Luke 11:13; John 14:15-26; John 16:12-15; Acts 2:38; Romans 8:26; Romans 15:13; 1 Corinthians 6:19; 2 Corinthians 3:17; Galatians 5:22-23 and Ephesians 1:13-14.

What does God's Holy Spirit do for us? What kind of disadvantage do we have if we try to "do" this Christian walk in our own strength?

4) Read Ephesians 2:14-19 and Revelation 7:9. God is in the process of saving people from every tribe on the face of the planet, in order to create a new race of humanity. In what ways do our churches succeed and fail in reflecting this new reality?

5) God promises that he is working out a specific process in those of us who place our faith in Christ: conforming us into the image of His Son (Romans 8:29). How do you see that process playing out in your own life?

6) Before God's promise is fulfilled in the earth, Jesus says a host of calamities and wars must first happen around the planet (Matthew 24). False prophets and messiahs will come. Then, before Christ's second-coming, the Anti-Christ must be revealed. He will decree all must take his Mark. And he will lead a terrible time called the Tribulation. Are you taking Jesus' words seriously? How are you preparing for this time? Is it possible this could take place in our generation?

7) God is sovereign. The Bible says that we live, then die and then must be judged for how we lived. If God is Just, then all injustice must be judged and all righteousness will be rewarded. This means that no one is exempt from the all-knowing eyes of Christ. So, then, how should we live?

8) Jesus promises us the Renewal of All Things (Matthew 19:28-30). How can this promise change the way you think and live? What does it say about our failures in life? Take time to imagine this... Renewal.

9) What will work be like in God's coming kingdom? In the Story, it's stated that work and worship will combine into a joyous and fulfilling experience. Allow me to share a story about this...

I had finished writing this book when my 8 year old son came to me and asked, "Daddy... what will it be like in heaven and on the new earth?" You have to understand that my son is a deep thinker and sometimes comes up with questions that cause me to go to God in prayer before answering them [laughing]! So, we had a discussion about what our experience in God's kingdom would be like. We talked about how there will be no more pain, suffering and death; and how we will have bodies like Jesus. We'll basically be superheroes—in the sense that Jesus walked on water, flew, controlled the elements, teleported from place to place, could read people's minds, etc... We too would be able to do similar things.

Needless to say, my son was super excited about the possibilities. And then he quieted down and had a somber look on his face.

"Daddy?"

"Yes, Son."

"Will we have to do work in heaven and on the new earth?"

There it was... You see, my son doesn't really like to do work... well, at least *certain kinds* of work.

"Sure, we'll have work to do," I replied. *"You think we're just going to sit around all day and do nothing?"*

He chuckled before continuing. "No.... but will the work be... boring?"

There it was again... the heart of the matter.

"No," I replied. "The work that we'll be doing definitely won't be boring."

"How do you know?" he pressed.

"Because we will be able to do everything God created us to do. We will be able to use all of our gifts and talents for his glory without any type of fear or hesitation or miscommunication."

He thought about it for a bit and then asked, "Will there be sports in heaven and on the new earth? You know I like sports."

My response after laughing... "I don't see why there wouldn't be."

After a couple minutes more, he was off to a completely different topic. No doubt one day we will revisit our talk of "the world to come." But he hit the nail right on the head! Isn't that what **we all** are wondering? Will it be boring in heaven? Will we just be sitting down on white puffy clouds with harps? Will we be engaged in one unending Sunday morning worship service?

You have to realize that "boring" is connected to our falling away from God's grace. While the Bible reveals some of what we will be doing and is silent on the major aspects, it does provide hints. One such hint is found in Matthew 25:14-30. Here, Jesus gives the parable of the Talents. While an entire book could be written on this parable alone, let me just point out one aspect as it relates to work—the Master's response to two of his servants:

"Well done, good and faithful servant. You have been faithful over a little; I will set you over much. Enter into the joy of your master."

The talents and resources God gives us while we are here on earth are "FEW" compared to what he has in store for us in his coming kingdom! When Jesus talks about setting us over much, it is directly connected to the joy of God. So, the responsibilities that will be our "work" will be connected to JOY! I think a **hallelujah** right here is appropriate!

I don't know about you, but there have been several times in my life where I have worked jobs that I absolutely loved. Jobs where I couldn't believe I was being paid to do that particular kind of work. Jobs where all of my gifts and talents were able to be used! (And then there were jobs where this was not the case. Where every day seemed like drudgery and I couldn't stop looking at the clock and couldn't wait for Friday to come.)

The indication is that our time on earth is a testing of our faithfulness. It is a testing of our character. It is preparation for the eternal work God desires to give us. A work that will span the new heaven, the new earth and the new universe beyond. So, when you think about being in heaven for all eternity, realize that in a state of eternal perfection, there is no room for boredom. What God has waiting for us will be worth the wait! What kind of work will you be doing in the coming kingdom?

10) What is God's central eternal purpose? What is your purpose? Which purpose are you living for? What Scriptures can you find to help you with the process of exchanging your purpose for God's? *(Take a look at Ephesians 3:8-12 and Revelation 14:6-7 to begin.)*

CLOSING THOUGHTS ON THE GOSPEL OF JESUS

1) There are 3 types of death mentioned in the Bible. Due to sin we are born spiritually dead. Then we will die physically. Then we will face eternal (second) death. How does Jesus Christ rectify our predicament?

2) All humans, no mater their status in life, have a heart disease. What do you think about the following quote by Ravi Zacharias?

"God didn't come to make bad people good. He came to make dead people live."

3) What is the worldview lens through which you view your life? How do you evaluate it? What is the standard by which you evaluate your worldview? Do you just take what society feeds you as "normal" or do you search beneath the surface for the truth?

4) What do you think of the following quote by C.S. Lewis?

"Christianity, if false, is of no importance, and if true, is of infinite importance. The only thing it cannot be is moderately important."

5) The Bible declares that the very presence of the universe is evidence of God's existence (Psalm 19:1). We are without excuse (Romans 1:20-25). Why do people continually try to deny God's existence?

6) From the expanses of the universe, down to the smallest elements of creation, God has provided evidence of his existence. Whether it's the extreme specificity of the universe, the existence of language in our DNA or the wondrous properties of the <u>cell adhesion molecule protein</u> **<u>Laminin</u>**. Everywhere we look, God's fingerprint can be seen. *Take some time to research these examples and others.*

7) If the universe was designed, then who is the Designer? What were we designed for? And can we know this Designer for ourselves? The Bible states that God is the Designer and he *wants* us to know him!

8) The Good News is that Jesus Christ does for us what we cannot do for ourselves. How does this free us to live a life that is unhindered?

9) The apostles were given every opportunity to turn away from the gospel. They were persecuted, imprisoned and eventually martyred for their faith in Christ. Only John died a natural death. They were convinced that Jesus was the Savior of the world because of one crucial experience: they encountered Jesus Christ—resurrected from the dead! His resurrection changed everything for them! <u>How can focusing on Christ's resurrection change how you face the world?</u>

10) Does Jesus being resurrected change everything? Not just in eternity, but also here-and-now? What is Christ resurrecting us for?

11) If the greatest enemy to humanity is death, how does Jesus overcoming death, hell and the grave free us up to do God's will?

12) Revisit the questions on page 90 and work your way through them.

13) Does the promise of resurrection mean you will never have to go

through struggles in life? How does the promise empower you to meet life's challenges head on?

14) Which earth are you living for? The current (old) earth or the (new) earth which is to come?

15) How do you view salvation? Is it "life after you die"? Or does it affect who you are... now?

Take a moment to find a quiet place to do the following exercise:

Imagine yourself standing next to an incredibly wide and powerful raging river. Hear the sound of the rushing water. See the plant and animal life all around its banks and in the stream itself. Look to your left—where the water is flowing from—and realize that the river stretches back further than your eyes can see. Now, look to your right and see that it again stretches into the unknown distance.

This river represents the Eternal Salvation God offers us. It has no beginning and it has no ending because it flows from the very life-force of Christ himself (John 17:3). Now, step into the river... or dive in if you prefer. Feel its current all around you. Don't fight the flow of the water. The more you do, the increasingly tired you will become.

Let the water sweep over you. Allow it to flow through you and take you on a journey that will never end. Don't be afraid of being drowned. This is the life-giving water Jesus talked about with the Samaritan woman in John 4:13-14. It is also the river Jesus said would flow out of our bellies, in John 7:38, so we can impact those around us. So, being overcome by the flowing water of *this* river actually gives *more* life! Every river eventually leads to a larger body of water. This one is no different. Eternity awaits.

God brings each of us to the banks of his river. All of us, from different backgrounds and times in history, are given an opportunity to enter the expansive, raging, flowing current of Salvation. With that opportunity comes the ability to refuse. We can choose to stay on the bank where it's dry. But, to do so means to never experience the true life which flows in, around and through a person who has entered the river.

EPILOGUE: THOUGHTS ON SATAN'S GREAT DECEPTION

1) What do you think of the following quote by C.S. Lewis?

"There are two equal and opposite errors into which our race can fall about the devils. One is to disbelieve in their existence. The other is to believe and to feel an excessive and unhealthy interest in them. They themselves are equally pleased with both errors."

2) Satan has various modes of deceptions. The first is to make people believe he does not exist. What other aspects can you come up with?

3) The Bible says that Satan can disguise himself as an angel of light (2 Corinthians 11:14). The Bible also says that he is the Father of lies (John 8:44). How then can we tell the difference between Satan's lies and God's truth? (Refer to 1 John 4:1-6)

4) Why does Satan want us to believe we are not made in God's image?

5) Consider the following quote:

*"It is hard for us to picture "forever" from this particular vantage point of time and space. And that is **precisely** what the devil is counting on!"*

Why does Satan want us to **NOT** focus on "forever?" How does this affect our decision making? Do we realize that "forever" is a *whole lot longer* than the years we spend in this life?

6) One of Satan's greatest lies is that **there is nothing beyond death.** That once we die, all existence ceases. That we are nothing more than fleshly machines that will one day break down. So, since human life does not exist beyond death, we don't have to fear judgment, because there is no God. So, we can be free to live however we want, for tomorrow we die!

Many people have swallowed this lie. In doing so, they have been blinded to the truth that it is appointed for us to live, then die and then face judgment (Hebrews 9:27).

Even the first law of thermodynamics goes against the lie that Satan has so many believing. It demonstrates that the energy of a closed system can't be created or destroyed, but only transformed. In other words, you can't add to it nor detract from it once it's created. *This is very interesting because in a very real sense, each human being is a walking, talking, thinking "closed system."* We are encased in flesh and blood. So, if our bodies are made up of matter (one form of energy) and we have consciousness/ spirit (another form of energy), then when we die, the energy that makes up "**us**" must go somewhere!

The Bible reveals that life does continue after we die. We **do** go somewhere... we go to stand before God for judgment. What other lies does Satan try to get us to believe?

ARE YOU LIVING BY THE RESURRECTION?

Hopefully this Study Guide has helped to stimulate your thinking and passion around understanding God's purpose for your life and for humanity as a whole. While we need to have introspection and be challenged, we also need to move from introspection to action. Here are some closing thoughts for this Study Guide which speaks to the practicality of living by the resurrection with those who may be adversarial towards us.

At first, the message of Jesus Christ being the Messiah, was given to the Jews. As they began to believe, many thought the message was ONLY for the Jewish nation. However, God made it abundantly clear through the ministry of the apostles Peter and Paul, that the message of the gospel was to be spread around the world. In truth, it was available to any and all who would believe, because all persons were in need of a Savior, since being under the power of sin, death and the devil. So, the message of Jesus' crucifixion and resurrection was shared with as many people groups as possible... even with those who were considered to be enemies of the Jewish people or those who the Jews looked down on.

"I now realize how true it is that God does not show favoritism but accepts from every nation the one who fears him and does what is right." - Apostle Peter at Cornelius' home (Acts 10:34-35)

Living by the resurrection means that we change our focus on how we view the world and our place within it. It means loving and praying for our enemies. It means living according to Ephesians 6 which tells us that though we struggle with other humans, our **PRIMARY** struggle in life is **NOT** against them, but against invisible forces of evil working behind the scenes to keep us at each other's throats.

These forces work overtime to make us think that our primary enemy is of a different ethnicity, or gender, or class, or nationality. Satan keeps us focused on each other so that he may roam freely about, unawares, destroying as many lives as possible. The truth is, the entire world is under the power of the devil. God desires to set men and women, boys and girls free. He has called us, as his children and ambassadors to *see differently, think differently and to live differently.* Jesus has called us to Live by his resurrection!

Living by the resurrection means Galatians 2:20 becomes increasingly real in our life.

"I have been crucified with Christ and I no longer live, but Christ lives in me. The life I now live in the body, I live by faith in the Son of God, who loved me and gave himself for me."

Realize that God will call us to suffer some things for his sake. Christ's suffering was redemptive in order to save many. We, as part of his body, must maintain this same viewpoint. When we suffer, as a Christian, do not take it as a personal attack. (I know it's easier said than done.) However, it is crucial that we see it as a redemptive act God will use to help draw the lost to Jesus.

Understand that there cannot be a resurrection if there is not first a crucifixion. Though we are now citizens of heaven, there are still very real aspects to our thought-life and personality which need to die in order for Christ's resurrection life to burst forth in us as a new way to live, think and act!

I will end with Philippians 3: 10-12 where the apostle Paul expresses his deepest desire.

"10I want to know Christ—yes, to know the power of his resurrection and participation in his sufferings, becoming like him in his death, 11and so, somehow, attaining to the resurrection from the dead. 12Not that I have already obtained all this, or have already arrived at my goal, but I press on to take hold of that for which Christ Jesus took hold of me."

May these words become our greatest desire as well! If they do, then God will be able to use us in ways we can't even imagine. And we will know him at a depth most people rarely dream is possible. We will be able to accomplish God's purpose for us in *this* life, and the eternal state of our existence will be secured in Christ for the ages which are to come.

HOW TO STUDY THE BIBLE

Many people feel that the Bible, because of its length, among a number of other reasons, is too intimidating and complex a book to really know and understand. They are unsure of how to dive into the Story. However, the Bible is God's Word to us, which reveals truth about his purposes and what he desires of us as his creation. God does not want us to remain ignorant of his Word.

To be a follower of Christ and not know his Word is to be at a clear disadvantage in life. The Bible lets us know what God desires and requires of us; and the blessings, provisions and power he makes available to us. It also gives us a clear understanding of the forces at work against us; and reveals our origin and the glorious future which awaits us.

James 1:22 tells us not to *just* listen to the Word, but more importantly, we are to put God's Word into *action*. 2 Timothy 2:15 tells us to study God's Word intently so we can present ourselves before him as approved and unashamed. Joshua 1:8 tells us to meditate on God's Word day and night so we will do as it says and be guided to the success and prosperity God has for us. And Acts 17: 11-12 tells us about the Berean Jews who received the gospel with great eagerness and examined the Scriptures daily to make sure they were true!

It is not enough to just read a few verses here and there—like taking a "spiritual" vitamin once a day. The Bible is meant to be a feast: read, studied, meditated upon, and put into action. God wants us to become students of his Word so he can work in us for his glory and our good!

Here are 7 ways to dive deeper into the Bible:

One: Pray *before* you read.

I Corinthians 2:14 states, "The natural person does not accept the things of the Spirit of God, for they are folly to him, and he is not able to understand them because they are spiritually discerned." When you read the Bible, always start with asking God to open your understanding and to guide you by his Spirit. Don't just expect that you can handle what you read with your own logic.

Two: Have access to a good Study Bible, Bible Dictionary, Concordance, several different translations, and a Commentary.

This may seem like a lot, but it is necessary in order to help us gain a better understanding of Scripture. There are several reasons to have these things. *1. You can look up the definitions of key terms, places or things with the Bible Dictionary. 2. You can look up a key word in its original language with the Concordance, to get a better understanding of what it means. 3. Several translations can help you overcome "wording" issues, so you can get a clearer understanding of the verse and passages. 4. A commentary provides background information to help you understand the context of what was happening at the time the passage was written.*

You have to understand that when things are translated from one language to another, some aspects may be hidden due to the limitations of the new language. For example, in the English language, the word LOVE means basically one thing. However, in the Hebrew and Greek (the original languages the Old and New Testaments were written in) the word LOVE has a number of different tenses, nuances, and levels.

A good set of Bible translations to have include: King James, New King James, the NIV, ESV, CEV, the Message, NLT, and the Amplified Bible. Some great Bible apps and websites for your smart phone are YouVersion, Accordance, Blue Letter Bible and Logos. And when you read a particular passage, read it in several different translations.

Remember, the Bible is meant to be read, studied, meditated upon and put into action! It is not meant to simply be read like any other book.

Three: Read the Bible based on a: Theme, Book, Word Study, and/or Plan.

Perhaps you want to focus on a specific theme, like Salvation or Repentance. Use your Bible Dictionary, Concordance, (or even Google) to find the Scriptures dealing with the theme you are interested in.

Perhaps you want to simply pick a book of the Bible and read it in its entirety. There are 66 books in the Bible. The Old Testament has 39 and the New Testament has 27. They are broken down into different genres: Historical, The Law, Wisdom, Psalms, Prophecy, Apocalyptic, Gospel and Epistles. There are a lot of books to choose from.

Perhaps you want to do a Word Study on a specific word. For example: SIN. You can look up the word in your Concordance and see every Scripture in the Bible where that word is used. You can also see the definition of the word in its original language.

Perhaps you want to get a reading plan. A popular one is "Read the Bible in a Year." There are a number of reading plans, some focusing on themes, which will help you dive deeper into the Holy Scriptures.

Four: Pray the Scriptures.

Read God's Word prayerfully. And make it a point, when you pray throughout your day, that you <u>include God's Word in your prayer.</u> Jesus wants us to abide in him and for his Word to abide in us (John 15:7). God responds to his Word and seeks to perform it, when we speak and act upon it in faith (Jeremiah 1:12). Also, as you pray God's Word, it begins to work on you as it challenges you to come to God in humble submission (Isaiah 26:3; Philippians 4: 6-7). A good place to start is the prayer Jesus taught his disciples (Matthew 6: 5-15; Luke 11: 1-4).

Five: Understand that Context is Key!

It is a dangerous thing to take a single verse in isolation without considering the passages which surround it. This can lead to misinterpretation. You must read God's word in context. You can start by reading the few verses before and after the one you want to focus on.

Then you can read the entire chapter in which the verse is located. You may then even need to read the entire book.

As you read, ask these questions to gain a better sense of context: *Who is the writer talking to? What was going on at that time? What is the writer trying to convey? What was the response of the hearers?* Note that study Bibles often include introductions, articles and footnotes for each book, which will help you understand context.

We make a mistake when we read a verse or passage, without understanding the context, and immediately apply our <u>modern day logic and sensibilities</u> to it.

For example: Jesus told his disciples that, *"it is easier for a camel to go through the eye of a needle than for a rich person to be saved." The disciples were astonished and replied, "Who then can be saved?"*

<u>Without knowing context, when we hear "the eye of a needle," we may immediately think of a sewing needle that a thread goes through.</u> However, after researching the context of that statement (through the use of a commentary, Bible dictionary, etc), you will discover that *"the eye of a needle"* is the name for a short, narrow passageway. A person usually used their camels to carry people and luggage. However, the camel was too wide and tall to go through the passageway. So, the luggage would have to be taken off and the camel would have to lower itself on its knees and crawl through the passageway to the other side. Then it could stand up again and continue its journey.

So, Jesus is saying that it is easier for a camel to humble itself than it is for a rich person to be saved. Why? Because to be saved, a person must realize that they NEED saving and then humble themselves before God so he can DO the saving. Certain rich people are not humble because their money affords them whatever they want in life. So, they go where they want, eat what they want, buy what they want and treat people any way they want, all because they are rich, and they will fight to maintain their wealth at all costs. Humility is not in the vocabulary of these types of rich people, so it is incredibly difficult for them to be saved.

So, what is Jesus getting at? <u>Your riches cannot secure you an eternal spot in heaven with God</u>. Only humbling yourself before God can. However, if you never search for the context of the passage you are reading, you will never come to that conclusion. And when you apply the context to your own life, in our modern-day setting, you see all sorts of things, but especially the need to humble (lower) yourself before God who is the source of your life and your blessings. You will also see the need to use any riches you may have been given in a way that brings honor to God and helps others.

Six: When possible, take the previous steps and put them into action in a Bible Study group with fellow Christians.

Each of us has a particular perspective on life. The Bible says that followers of Christ are part of his body. When we study God's Word together and share what we see (and even what we don't understand), we give God the opportunity to open up his Word among us in a special way. There is nothing quite like studying, researching, meditating on, and determining how to put a passage into action **together**. Jesus says in Matthew 18:20, "For where two or three gather in my name, I am there with them."

Seven: Consistency in Bible engagement is key!

The Bible is very much "food and drink" to the follower of Christ. How often do you eat within a given day or week? How consistent is your nutritional intake? Do you only eat a couple of times a week? Probably not. And when you *do* eat, are you eating junk food, which tears your body down, or nutritious meals which strengthens your body and mind?

If you want your body and mind to be strong, then you must be consistent about eating right (and exercising). If this is the case in the natural, how does consistency affect you in the spiritual? Even Jesus said, "Man shall not live on bread alone, but on every word that comes from the mouth of God" (Matthew 4:4). An engagement study produced by *Back to the Bible* revealed that life-change happens when a person consistently reads Scripture 4 or more times a week. How often do you engage? Your consistency matters!

DEFINITION OF TERMS

Sinner

A person who is unregenerate (not renewed in heart and mind, not reborn in spirit, spiritually dead) and therefore lost and separated from God by their fallen sin-nature.

Saint

A person who has yielded their life to Christ and has been redeemed (to buy back or recover by payment) and reconciled to God by the Blood of Jesus, which he shed as a sin-cleansing sacrifice on the cross.

Repentance

A person must repent before they can be saved. They cannot be saved by God if they believe they have done nothing wrong. Repentance is to realize and acknowledge that one is a sinner. A person must see that their sins separate them from God, be sorrowful for their sinfulness and ask God for forgiveness through Jesus Christ. Then, they must also be determined to turn away from their sinful lifestyle and go in the direction God desires for them.

Faith

Belief, confidence, trust and reliance in Jesus Christ and his Word as true. Faith is confidence in God to keep his promises to us. Because we believe, trust and rely on God's Word as true, we also make daily decisions and actions based on our relationship with Christ. Genuine faith is not "blind" and does **not** mean: believing something without proof. God provides evidence through his Word, the indwelling of his Holy Spirit, the physical creation all around us and intervention in our circumstances to let us know that he can be trusted.

Salvation

The process by which God does for us what we cannot do for ourselves. He saves us from the wrath of our sins, the power of sin, death, hell, grave and the empire of Satan. God takes us out of darkness and delivers us into his Kingdom of light and brings us into a new, full, complete-yet-growing, relationship with himself, through his eternal Son, Jesus. He takes us in our "deadness" and makes us alive in Christ!

Regeneration

In John 3, Jesus said we must be born again if we are to see and enter the Kingdom of God. This is the process of conversion by which a sinner is made alive by the indwelling of the Holy Spirit. Scripture teaches that in Christ, old things have passed away and all things have been made new.

Justification

God grants the pardon of sin and the promise of eternal life based on our faith in Jesus Christ as his Son and our Savior. Justification cannot be earned by our "good" works. It is given in response to our trusting in the finished work of Jesus Christ (crucifixion and resurrection).

Propitiation

A two-part act that involves appeasing the wrath of God, who is offended by our sinful state, and being reconciled into a right relationship with God. Both of these aspects are made possible through the crucifixion and resurrection of Jesus Christ.

Sanctification

The process by which God, through the power of the Holy Spirit and the Word, conforms us into the image of his Son, Jesus. This is the progressive, ongoing work of transformation God is engaged in from the time we receive his salvation. It will continue until the day that we die. Our job is to yield ourselves to God's working in our lives.

Grace

God's unmerited favor towards us. When God gives us his grace, it is not based on "following the rules" or our own innate goodness. God's grace is based solely on his prerogative and flows from his love for us.

The Gospel

Good News about the salvation (new life) God brings through Jesus Christ for humanity's broken state of existence.

Righteousness

God imputed righteousness to Abraham because he believed and trusted God at his Word. Righteousness and being called "righteous" is when you take God at his word and live in the way he wants you to live. It is through the power of Christ that we are enabled to live in such fashion.

Wickedness

Living in a way that displeases God. This includes, but is not limited to, the obvious sins of murder, lying, cheating, stealing, sexual immorality, etc. Wickedness can also include doing things we would consider "good." The problem is that wickedness is rooted in our choosing to disbelieve God and his Word. So, when we act with no regard for God, even when we do "good" things, our actions can still be considered wicked at the internal motivational level because we do not seek to please and honor God through our decision-making.

Sin

This word means "to miss the mark." It is applied to the reality that God has a standard for humanity, and we each constantly miss that standard due to our own estimations of what is right and wrong, good and evil. We are disobedient in ways that are both complicit and unconscious. Sin is not just the things we do which go against God's Word. It is also when we don't do what God says we should do.

The sinful things we do are symptoms of the deeper issue of sin. Sin is at the core of who we are. It was introduced into the human race and the world with the disobedience of the first humans, Adam and Eve. When they chose to disobey the only rule God gave them (not to eat from the Tree of the Knowledge of Good and Evil), Sin entered humanity and forever marred us. This is why we so desperately need Jesus.

ARTICLES OF FAITH

INTRODUCTION

The Articles of Faith present the heart of what we believe as Christians (in particular) and as Baptists (specifically). They can be found in the back of most Baptist hymnals and on a variety of Baptist websites, such as the National Baptist Convention, USA Incorporated.

These Articles are the key aspects of our faith and are commonly held —at least in part—by many denominations. Scripture states in 1 Peter 3:15, "...Always be prepared to give an answer to everyone who asks you to give the reason for the hope that you have. But do this with gentleness and respect..."

Oftentimes, those who profess to be believers in Christ have difficulty explaining **what** they believe and **why** they believe it. To say we have faith is one thing. To have an **informed faith**—which is further built on biblical understanding—is quite another. This is why studying the Articles of Faith is important!

Each Article serves as a piece of the spiritual foundation upon which we stand. Romans 10:17 tells us that *"Faith comes by hearing the Word of God."* The more we hear and understand, the stronger our faith becomes. And the Articles of Faith help take broad concepts (faith and God's Kingdom) and break it down into manageable parts for our spiritual consumption.

Finally, in Matthew 13:19 Jesus states: *"When anyone hears the message about the kingdom and does not understand it, the evil one comes and snatches away what was sown in their heart. This is the seed sown along the path."* What we should seek in our Christian journey is **understanding**. Studying the Articles of Faith, will enable us to hold onto God's Good News and put it into practice in our everyday lives.

The Bible was written by 40 authors over the course of 1500 years, in 3 languages and on 3 continents. It was written by kings, shepherds, scholars, and fishermen and has a consistent theme and teachings from beginning to end. There are prophecies concerning the Messiah that were written hundreds of years before Jesus Christ was born and fulfilled them. There is not one clear contradiction in the Bible. Many historical and archaeological findings support the accuracy and reliability of Scripture. The Bible has spoken accurately about many areas of science long before human discoveries were made.

THE ARTICLES OF FAITH

1. The Scriptures. We believe that the Holy Bible was written by men divinely inspired, and is a perfect treasure of heavenly instruction; that it has God for its author, salvation for its end, and truth without any mixture of error for its matter; that it reveals the principles by which God will judge us, and therefore is, and shall remain to the end of the world, the true center of Christian union, and the supreme standard by which all human conduct, creeds, and opinions shall be tried.

*2 Timothy 2:15   *2 Timothy 3:16-17   *2 Peter 1:20-21
*Matthew 19:4-5   *Luke 4: 16-21   *Acts 18:28

2. The True God. We believe the Scriptures teach that there is one, and only one, living and true God, an infinite, intelligent Spirit, whose name is Jehovah, the Maker and Supreme Ruler of heaven and earth; inexpressibly glorious in holiness, and worthy of all possible honor, confidence and love; that in the unity of the Godhead there are three persons, the Father, the Son, and the Holy Ghost; equal in every divine perfection, and executing distinct but harmonious offices in the great work of redemption.

*Genesis 1:1-2, 26 *Matthew 3:16-17   *Matthew 17:1-5
*John 1: 1-5   *John 14: 15-21   *John 16: 12-15
*Colossians 1:15-20

3. The Fall of Man. We believe the Scriptures teach that Man was created in holiness, under the law of his Maker; but by voluntary transgressions fell from that holy and happy state; in consequence of which all mankind are now sinners, not by constraint but choice; being by nature utterly void of that holiness required by the law of God, positively inclined to evil; and therefore under just condemnation to eternal ruin, without defense or excuse.

*Genesis 1:26-30   *Genesis 2:15-25   *Genesis 3:1-24
*Genesis 6: 5-8   *Psalm 51:5   *Jeremiah 17:9
*Romans 5: 12, 19 *Romans 8: 20-22

4. The Way of Salvation. We believe that the Scriptures teach that the salvation of sinners is wholly of grace; through the mediatorial offices of the Son of God; who by the appointment of the Father, freely took upon him our nature, yet without sin; honored the divine law by his personal obedience, and by his death made a full atonement for our sins; that having risen from the dead, he is now enthroned in heaven; and uniting in his wonderful person the tenderest sympathies with divine perfections, he is in every way qualified to be a suitable, a compassionate, and an all-sufficient Savior.

*John 1: 29   *John 3: 14-21   *John 20: 29
*Romans 10:1-4, 8-13   *Ephesians 2: 1-9
*Ephesians 1:7   *Philippians 2: 5-11
*Hebrews 2: 14-18 *Hebrews 4: 14-16   *Hebrews 9: 27-28

5. Justification. We believe the Scriptures teach that the great Gospel blessing which Christ secures to such as believe in him is justification; that justification includes the pardon of sin, and the promise of eternal life on principles of righteousness; that it is bestowed, not in consideration of any works of righteousness which we have done, but solely through faith in the Redeemer's blood; by virtue of which faith his perfect righteousness is freely imputed to us of God; that it brings us into a state of most blessed peace and favor with God, and secures every other blessing needful for time and eternity.

*Acts 13: 36-39   *Romans 3: 19-26   *Romans 5: 1-2
*Romans 4: 23   *Romans 8: 28-30   *2 Corinthians 5: 21
*Galatians 2: 11-16, 20-21   *Hebrews 9: 22-10:4

6. The Freeness of Salvation. We believe that the Scriptures teach that the blessings of salvation are made free to all by the Gospel; that it is the immediate duty of all to accept them by cordial, penitent and obedient faith; and that nothing prevents the salvation of the greatest sinner on earth, but his own determined depravity and voluntary rejection of the Gospel; which rejection involves him in an aggravated condemnation.

*John 3: 16-21   *Ephesians 2:8-9   *Romans 3: 21-26
*Romans 4: 1-5   *Romans 5:15-17   *John 1: 12

7. Regeneration. We believe that the Scriptures teach that in order to be saved, sinners must be regenerated, or born again; that regeneration consists in giving a holy disposition to the mind that it is effected in a manner above our comprehension by the power of the Holy Spirit in connection with divine truth, so as to secure our voluntary obedience to the Gospel; and that its proper evidence appears in the holy fruits of repentance and faith, and newness of life.

Regeneration	Christian Mind	Evidence
*John 1: 11-13	*Philippians 2:5; 4:6-8	*Galatians 5: 16-26
*John 3: 3-8	*Romans 12:2	*Ephesians 3: 17-19
*Romans 10: 8-10	*Ephesians 4:22-32	*Colossians 2: 6-7
*1 Peter 1:3	*Isaiah 26:3	*Colossians 3: 9-10
*2 Corinthians 5: 17-18	*John 15:5	*1 Peter 1: 22-23
*2 Corinthians 3:18	*Titus 3: 3-7	*Ephesians 2: 1-10

8. Repentance and Faith. We believe the Scriptures teach that repentance and faith are sacred duties, and also inseparable graces, wrought in our souls by the regenerating Spirit of God; whereby being deeply convinced of our guilt, danger and helplessness and of the way of salvation by Christ, we turn to God with unfeigned contrition, confession, and supplication for mercy; at the same time heartily receiving the Lord Jesus Christ as our prophet, priest, and king, and relying on him alone as the only and all-sufficient Savior.

*Matthew 3: 1-2	*Luke 3: 8	*Matthew 4: 17
*Luke 24: 45-47	*Mark 1: 14-15	*Romans 12: 3
*Luke 5: 27-32	*Hebrews 12: 1-2	*Matthew 12: 41
*Luke 13: 1-5		

9. God's Purpose of Grace. We believe the Scriptures teach that election is the eternal purpose of God, according to which he graciously regenerates, sanctifies and saves sinners; that being perfectly consistent with the free agency of man, it comprehends all the means in connection with the end; that it is a most glorious display of God's sovereign goodness, being infinitely free, wise, holy and unchangeable; that it utterly excludes boasting and promotes humility, love, prayer, praise, trust in God, and active imitation of his free mercy; that it encourages the use of means in the highest degree; that it may be ascertained by its effects in all who truly believe the Gospel; that it is the foundation of Christian assurance; and that to ascertain it with regard to ourselves demands and deserves the utmost diligence.

*Ephesians 2: 1-10	*Romans 8: 28-30	*2 Corinthians 12: 8-9
*Romans 3: 20-24	*Acts 6: 8	*James 4: 6
*John 6: 44		

10. Sanctification. We believe the Scriptures teach that Sanctification is the process by which, according to the will of God, we are made partakers of his holiness; that it is a progressive work; that it is begun in regeneration; and that it is carried on in the hearts of believers by the presence and power of the Holy Spirit, the Sealer and Comforter, in the continual use of the appointed means especially the word of God, self-examination, self-denial, watchfulness, and prayer.

*1 Thessalonians 5: 23 *John 17: 17 *2 Timothy 2: 14-26
*Galatians 2: 20 *1 Corinthians 6: 9-11
*Hebrews 10: 11-18 *Philippians 1: 6 *Romans 12: 1-2

11. Perseverance of the Saints. We believe the Scriptures teach that such only are real believers as endure to the end; that their persevering attachment to Christ is the grand mark which distinguishes them from superficial professors; that a special Providence watches over their welfare; and they are kept by the power of God through faith unto salvation. A Christian's purpose is to walk with Jesus every day of our life and allow God to conform us to the image of Christ.

*John 6: 60-69 *John 10: 27-30 *Romans 8: 16-17, 38-39
*1 Peter 4: 12-19 *Revelation 2: 7, 11, 17, 26-29; 3: 5, 12, 21

12. The Law and Gospel. We believe the Scriptures teach that the Law of God is the eternal and unchangeable rule of his moral government; that it is holy, just and good; and that the inability which the Scriptures ascribe to fallen men to fulfill its precepts, arise entirely from their love of sin; to deliver them from which, and to restore them through a Mediator to unfeigned obedience to the holy Law, is one great end of the Gospel, and of the Means of Grace connected with the establishment of the visible church.

*2 Corinthians 5: 21 *Galatians 3: 19-25 *Numbers 23: 19
*Hebrews 13: 8 *James 1: 18 *John 3: 18-21
*Romans 7: 18-25

13. A Gospel Church. We believe the Scriptures teach that a visible church of Christ is a congregation of baptized believers, associated by covenant in the faith and fellowship of the Gospel; observing the ordinances of Christ; governed by his laws; and exercising the gifts, rights, and privileges invested in them by His Word; that its only scriptural officers are Bishops or Pastors, and Deacons whose Qualifications, claims and duties are defined in the Epistles to Timothy and Titus.

*Matthew 16: 18   *Acts 2: 40-47   *Ephesians 4: 5
*I Corinthians 13 *I Corinthians 12: 4 *I Timothy 3: 1-13
*Titus 1: 5-9

14. Baptism and the Lord's Supper. We believe the Scriptures teach that Christian baptism is the immersion in water of a believer, into the name of the Father, and Son, and Holy Ghost; to show forth in a solemn and beautiful emblem, our faith in the crucified, buried, and risen Savior, with its effect, in our death to sin and resurrection to a new life; that it is prerequisite to the privileges of a church relation; and to the Lord's Supper, in which the members of the church, by the sacred use of bread and wine, are to commemorate together the dying love of Christ; preceded always by solemn self-examination.

*Matthew 3: 13-17 *Mark 1: 9-10   *Matthew 28: 19
*Mark 1: 4, 5   *Mark 16: 16   *Acts 2: 38; 8: 35-38
*Romans 6: 3-6   *I Corinthians 12: 13 *Galatians 3: 27
*I Corinthians 11: 23-25   *Luke 22: 19

15. The Christian Sabbath. We believe the Scriptures teach that the first day of the week is the Lord's Day, or Christian Sabbath, and is to be kept sacred to religious purposes, by abstaining from all secular labor and sinful recreations, by the devout observance of all the means of grace, both private and public, and by preparation for that rest that remains for the people of God. New Testament Believers are not under the Old Testament Law (Romans 6: 14; Galatians 3: 24-25; 2 Corinthians 3: 7, 11,

13; Hebrews 7: 12). Christ's resurrection was on the first day of the week (Matthew 28: 1). Jesus appeared on additional Sundays (John 20:26). Early Church met on Sundays regularly (Acts 20:7, 1 Corinthians 16:2)

*Mark 2: 27	*Colossians 2: 16-17	*Deuteronomy 5: 15
*Exodus 20: 11	*Acts 20: 7	*Acts 15: 1-29

16. Civil Government. We believe the Scriptures teach that civil government is of divine appointment, for the interest and good order of human society; and that magistrates are to be prayed for, conscientiously honored and obeyed; except only in things opposed to the will of our Lord Jesus Christ, who is the only Lord of the conscience, and the Prince of the Kings of the earth.

*Romans 13: 1-7   *1 Peter 2: 13-17   *Daniel 1: 1-9

17. Righteous and Wicked. We believe the Scriptures teach that there is a radical and essential difference between the righteous and the wicked; that such only as through faith are justified in the name of the Lord Jesus, and sanctified by the Spirit of our God, are truly righteous in his esteem; while all such as continue in impenitence and unbelief are in his sight wicked, and under the curse; and this distinction holds among men both in and after death.

*John 1: 9-13	*1 Cor 6: 9-11	*John 3: 16-21
*Romans 8: 8-11	*Hebrews 9: 27-28	*Revelation 20: 11-15
*Romans 14: 10-13	*Matthew 24: 31-46	*2 Corinthians 5: 10-11
*1 John 1: 9		

18. The World to Come. We believe the Scriptures teach that the end of the world is approaching; that at the last day, Christ will descend from heaven, and raise the dead from the grave for final retribution; that a solemn separation will then take place; that the wicked will be assigned to endless punishment, and the righteous to endless joy; and that this judgment will fix forever the final state of men in heaven or hell, on principles of righteousness.

*Matthew 25: 31-46   *1 Thessalonians 4: 13-18
*Revelation 20: 7-15   *Revelation 21: 1-11   *Revelation 22: 1-5

20 OLD TESTAMENT PROPHECIES ABOUT JESUS CHRIST

<u>The central focal point of the entire Bible is Jesus Christ.</u> From Genesis to Revelation, the Word of God centers on him. In John 5:39 Jesus told the religious leaders of his day, "You study the Scriptures diligently because you think that in them you have eternal life. These are the very Scriptures that testify about me, yet you refuse to come to me to have life."

The purpose of the Old Testament prophecies was to herald the coming of the Messiah (the One chosen as the Savior of the world). They would also be a litmus test, for those who knew them, to know whether or not someone who claimed to be the Messiah was in fact *the Messiah*.

According to a Youtube video on Probability Science, *the probability of 8 prophecies being fulfilled accidentally in the life of one person is: 1 in 10^{17} or 1 in 100,000,000,000,000,000. That's one in one hundred quadrillion!

Jesus Christ fulfilled over 300 Old Testament prophecies about who the Messiah would be. He has been the **only** person to do so.

<u>Here are two New Testament verses where Jesus addresses this truth:</u>

"For if you had believed Moses, you would have believed me: for he wrote of me." **- John 5:46**

"How foolish you are, how slow you are to believe everything the prophets said! Was it not necessary for the Messiah to suffer these things and then to enter his glory?" And Jesus explained to them what was said about himself in all the Scriptures, beginning with the books of Moses and the writings of all the prophets.... They said to each other, "Wasn't it like a fire burning in us when he talked to us on the road and explained the Scriptures to us?" **Luke 24: 25-27, 32**

Here are 20 Old Testament prophecies which Jesus Christ fulfilled.

ONE: Genesis 3:15. The Messiah would be the seed of the woman. This was fulfilled in Matthew 1:18-25; Luke 1:26-38 / 2:1-40; Romans 16:20; Galatians 4:4; Revelation 12:9, 17.

TWO: Genesis 12:3. The Messiah would be the descendant of Abraham through whom all nations would be blessed. This was fulfilled in Matthew 1:1-18; Acts 3: 24-26.

THREE: Genesis 22: 1-18. The Messiah would be a willing sacrifice. This was fulfilled in Matthew 16:20-23; Luke 23:32-43; John 3:14-21 / 6:51 / 19:11.

FOUR: Exodus 12: 1-51. The Messiah would be the Passover Lamb. This was fulfilled in Mark 14:1-2, 12-25; John 1:29-36 / 11:49-52 / 19:33-36; 1 Corinthians 5:7-8; 1 Peter 1:19.

FIVE: Numbers 21: 6-9. The Messiah would be lifted up. This was fulfilled in Matthew 27:32-54; Mark 15:16-39; Luke 23:26-47; John 3: 14-18 / 19:16-30.

SIX: Deuteronomy 18: 15-19. The Messiah would be a prophet like Moses. This was fulfilled in Matthew 13:57; Matthew 21:46; Luke 24:13-27; John 1:21-27; John 6:14; John 7:40-41; Acts 3:22 / 7:37, 51-53 / 28:28.

SEVEN: 2 Samuel 7: 12-16. The Messiah would be a descendant of David. This was fulfilled in Matthew 1:1; Luke 1:32-33; Acts 15: 15-16; Hebrews 1:5.

EIGHT: Psalm 2:1-12. The Messiah would be called God's Son. This was fulfilled in Mark 1:11; Luke 3:22; Acts 4:25-28 / 13:32-33; Hebrews 1:5 / 5:5.

NINE: Psalm 16:8-11. The Messiah would be resurrected. This was fulfilled in Matthew 28:1-7; Mark 16:1-8; Luke 24:1-12; John 20:1-10; Acts 2:22-32 / 13:35-37.

TEN: Psalm 22:1-31. The Messiah would be forsaken and pierced, but vindicated. This was fulfilled in Matthew 27: 39-46; Mark 15:25-34; John 19:24; Hebrews 2:12.

ELEVEN: Psalm 110:1-4. The Messiah would be greater than David. This was fulfilled in Matthew 22:42-45. Mark 12:35-37; Luke 20:41-44; Acts 2:34-36; 1 Corinthians 15:25-28; Hebrews 1:3, 13; Hebrews 4:14-5:10.

TWELVE: Psalm 118:22-24. The Messiah would be the rejected cornerstone. This was fulfilled in Matthew 21:42-44; Mark 12:10-11; Luke 20:17-18; Acts 4:9-12; Ephesians 2:20; 1 Peter 2:6-8.

THIRTEEN: Isaiah 7:14. The Messiah would be born of a virgin. This was fulfilled in Matthew 1:18-25. Luke 1:31-35.

FOURTEEN: Isaiah 9:6-7. The Messiah would be the Wonderful Counselor, Mighty God, Everlasting Father and Prince of Peace. This was fulfilled in Luke 1:32-33, 79 / 2:8-14; John 6:51; John 14:27; Acts 10:36; Romans 9:5; Colossians 2:3.

FIFTEEN: Micah 5:2. The Messiah would be born in Bethlehem. This was fulfilled in Matthew 2:1-6; John 7:40-43.

SIXTEEN: Hosea 11:1. The Messiah would be called out of Egypt. This was fulfilled in Matthew 2:13-15.

SEVENTEEN: Zechariah 9:9. The Messiah would come riding on a colt. This was fulfilled in Matthew 21:1-11.

144

EIGHTEEN: Zechariah 11:12-13. <u>The Messiah would be betrayed for thirty pieces of silver.</u> This was fulfilled in Matthew 26:14-16; Matthew 27:3-10.

NINETEEN: Zechariah 12:10. <u>The Messiah would be pierced.</u> This was fulfilled in John 19:31-37; Revelation 1:7.

TWENTY: Malachi 3:1. <u>The Messiah would be preceded by a messenger.</u> This was fulfilled in Matthew 11:10; Mark 1:1-8; Luke 1:76-80, John 1:19-29.

FOR FURTHER STUDY...

*Youtube video: "Jesus Historically Fulfilled Over 300 Prophecies... Accidentally?" by IntelligentFaith 315

*https://jewsforjesus.org/answers/top-40-most-helpful-messianic-prophecies/

*http://christinprophecy.org/articles/applying-the-science-of-probability-to-the-scriptures/

*Youtube video: "Jesus in the Old Testament" by Behold Israel.

7 SPIRITUAL DISCIPLINES

A person without discipline will never develop to his or her full potential. This truth applies to all areas of our life: physically, mentally, spiritually, emotionally, relationally, morally, financially and creatively. By discipline, I do not mean a form of correction or punishment when one breaks a rule. Rather, I am talking about the strategy a person uses to consistently train him or herself to do something in a controlled and habitual way.

A disciplined life means that a person opens themselves up to certain practices while closing themselves off from other ones. It is a narrowing of the life in order to increase focus upon an area in which you want to grow. It means making time for what is truly important. If the truth were told, many of us spend the majority of our time on earth doing everything but focusing on the most important aspect of our existence: our spiritual lives. To be clear, we are not meant to approach our relationship with God from an individualistic standpoint, but rather as a fellowship. True and lasting growth happens when we are consistently moving together in the same direction.

As Christians, the focus for all spiritual disciplines IS TO KNOW CHRIST. There is no other viable reason. Any other reason is secondary (like those who say, "Fasting can also help you lose weight.") But, how can we grow in Christ? Not just our knowledge *about* him, but more importantly our relationship WITH him? *(2 Peter 1:1-11)*

What spiritual disciplines, are found in the Scriptures that would be instrumental in helping us grow closer to Christ? Here are several:

Prayer | Meditation | Fasting | Bible Study | Fellowship |Worship | Rest

PRAYER

Jesus' disciples watched him pray on many occasions. On one particular day, (according to Luke 11) they couldn't hold in their urgent need and curiosity any longer. They came to him and said, "Lord, teach us to pray as John taught his disciples."

Many people avoid prayer because they feel uncomfortable praying. They don't know what to say or how to say it. But we can learn something from the disciples as they watched Jesus pray on a daily basis. One day, after Jesus had finished praying, these disciples said to him, "Lord, teach us to pray…" They choose not to remain in ignorance any longer! They saw something in Jesus that they knew they wanted but didn't have… and they asked him to help them acquire it. They didn't know how to pray, but they knew they needed to learn how to pray! And Jesus provided them with the best starting point.

Prayer may seem uncomfortable. But prayer can be taught. You can learn to pray. You can become confident in prayer because God wants you, as his child, to be able to pray to him… to talk with him. You see, prayer is communion with God. It is both talking to and listening to God. It is the primary mode of communication that God has established between him and us. Prayer is a direct line to heaven. So, to not pray or to pray ineffectively leaves us at a disadvantage in our Christian journey.

Jesus taught about the nature of prayer in Matthew 6. Please read the entire chapter when you get the chance. But, here's what Jesus specifically said to his disciples in Matthew 6:9-13.

9 In this manner, therefore, pray: Our Father in heaven, Hallowed be Your name.

10 Your kingdom come. Your will be done on earth as it is in heaven.

11 Give us this day our daily bread.

12 And forgive us our debts, as we forgive our debtors.

13 And do not lead us into temptation, but deliver us

from the evil one. For Yours is the kingdom and the power and the glory forever. Amen.

Jesus provides an order we should observe when we approach God. We shouldn't always rush into God's Presence immediately asking for what we want! Praying the Scriptures is another aspect of prayer.

You <u>can</u> learn and grow in the spiritual discipline of prayer!

MEDITATION

Meditation, in this sense, does not mean "emptying your mind of thoughts." Rather, it means focusing your mind and thoughtfulness on Scripture. God declared in Joshua 1:7-8, that he should "meditate on the Law day and night." Here, the "Law" means the Word that was available to Joshua at that time (Law of Moses). We now, have the Old and New Testaments to meditate on.

The Bible declares in Romans 15:4 that the Scriptures were written for our benefit, so we can learn from them. However, we cannot learn from what we do not know. Hence, knowledge of God is a key reason to meditate on God's Word. What you consistently place your focus on (meditate) has an effect on you. Your thoughts and actions are actually influenced by what you meditate on.

2 Corinthians 10:5 tells us to, "cast down every imagination which exalts itself against the knowledge of God, and to bring every thought captive in obedience to Christ." Meditating on God's Word helps you to "think about what you are thinking about" and brings your thoughts under subjection to God's thoughts.

Romans 12:2 tells us, "And do not be conformed to the world (its way of thinking and doing), but be transformed by the renewing of your mind, so you can prove what is that good and acceptable and perfect will of God." Meditation helps us to renew our mind from the faulty thinking we have had for so long, in order to help conform us into the image of Christ—which is what God the Father is doing within each Christian (Romans 8:29).

You <u>can</u> learn and grow in the spiritual discipline of meditation!

FASTING

The purpose of fasting is to go without eating, for a time, in order to focus more on God's Presence in our lives. It is a way to minimize the impulses of our human flesh in order to bring our spirit and the Holy Spirit within us to the forefront of our existence. Some use fasting as a way to draw closer to the Lord in their overall relationship. Others fast to draw closer to God in specific areas of their lives, for example, to help overcome anger issues. At other times fasting is used because one is seeking God's direction for a specific situation in their lives.

The Bible lets us know that if we are not careful, our stomach can become our god (Philippians 3:18-20). For many of us, much of our waking moments are filled with thoughts about what and when we are going to eat. To find out just how much we are influenced by our stomachs, embark on a fast. Jesus tells us that people who do not know God spend their time chasing after what they will eat, drink, and wear (Matthew 6:31-33). When one fasts, they "turn down their plate" and use that time to "eat and drink" Scripture. Not eating food must go hand in hand with an increase of your spiritual diet of prayer and Bible reading.

There are different types of "food" fasting. You can fast a single meal, each day for a period of days. You can do a 6am to 6pm fast for a number of days. You can also fast for a full 24 hours—and several days at that. Some fasts will include water; others will not. There is also a Daniel Fast (Daniel chapter 1; Daniel 10: 1-3) where you eat a restricted diet of vegetables and water.

Often, when you fast, your stomach and body will attempt to "rebel." Sometimes, when fasting, food will look and smell more enticing! You can have increased hunger pains as well. This is all a part of your body reacting to the usual timetable by which you frequently eat. Fasting often reveals just how much we live to eat—instead of eating to live. Fasting can also reveal (and increase) the depth of your character. You will notice how you treat people (and they will notice too)! If you are grumpy and irritable while fasting, then you have room to grow! (smile)

God may call you and I to fast in other areas of our lives for a time to draw closer to him: such as a media fast. If you live for television, movies, the news, music and all things social media, God may call you to restrict your access for a time in order to draw closer to him. Again, fasting from media will reveal quite a bit about who we are and where we place priority in our lives.

Fasting, of any type, enables us to slow down aspects of our busy schedules and routines in order to see and hear what we would normally miss. Remember, God often speaks in a still, small voice. His leading and direction can often be crowded out by the noise of our lives. Again, fasting must go hand in hand with an increase of your spiritual diet of prayer and Bible reading.

You <u>can</u> learn and grow in the spiritual discipline of fasting!

BIBLE STUDY

The Bible is God's heart and mind to humanity. Some call it a Love Letter from God. Others call it a manual: Basic Instructions Before Leaving Earth. It is both and more! By it we learn about the nature of reality, the depth of good and evil in the universe, what is important to God, how he operates with humanity, what he requires and desires from us, where we come from as a species, and where we are going for eternity.

Most importantly, through reading and studying the Bible, we learn about God's eternal Son, Jesus Christ—who he is to us and who we are to him. Please refer to the previous article in the appendix on How to Study the Bible for further information.

You <u>can</u> learn and grown in the spiritual discipline of Bible study!

FELLOWSHIP

Many of us may not think of this as a spiritual discipline, but fellowship—growing together—can be a spiritual discipline all its own. Contemporary

Christianity in America is mostly individualistic in nature, but this is not how things are confirmed in the Scriptures. From the Old to the New Testament, God makes clear that we need each other in order to grow. Salvation is both personal/individual and it is corporate.

"As iron sharpens iron, so a friend sharpens a friend." - Proverbs 27:17 (NLT)

"A person standing alone can be attacked and defeated, but two can stand back-to-back and conquer. Three are even better, for a triple-braided cord is not easily broken." - Ecclesiastes 4:12 (NLT)

"For where two or three gather together as my followers, I am there among them." - Matthew 18:20 (NLT)

"And let us not neglect our meeting together, as some people do, but encourage one another, especially now that the day of his return is drawing near." - Hebrews 10:25 (NLT)

There is an African proverb that states, "If you want to go fast—go alone. But if you want to go far—go together!" Our Christian walk was not made for us to "go it alone." We were created for a fellowship. We were made to follow Christ together with other like-minded believers!

The Bible declares in Ecclesiastes 9:11 that the race is not given to the swift. The Christian life is not a sprint. It is not a cross-country race. It's not even a marathon. It is a triathlon of sorts. There are hills and valleys, dry ground and waves, sunshine and rain, and the best way we make it to the finish line is TOGETHER.

Fellowship is the act of deliberately sharing your life with other believers in an effort to grow in Christ together. It's sharing a meal. It's sharing our hopes and dreams and failures. It's sharing God's Word. It's praying and singing together. It's being present for each other. It's standing in the gap and bringing each other before the Lord in prayer.

Fellowship is "doing life" together. It's having all things in common with each other. It's more than seeing each other on Sunday at a worship service. It's not about coming to the church building. It's being built up together **as** the Church. And each part needs the other. Fellowship is acknowledging that as Christ-followers, we are intricate parts of the body of Christ. We are all daughters and sons in the same Family of God.

You <u>can</u> learn and grow in the spiritual discipline of fellowship!

WORSHIP

John 4:23 states, "But an hour is coming, and now is, when the true worshipers will worship the Father in spirit and truth; for such people the Father seeks to be his worshipers."

Learning how to worship God is a spiritual discipline. At its heart, worship is about reflecting the love that God showers on us, back to him. It is coming before God with a sincere and open heart. It's about acknowledging God's sovereignty over your life and realizing his blessings in your life. Worship is an act of saying "thank you" to the One from whom all blessings flow. (James 1:17)

Worship is being truthful with God about your life and seeking his truth about who he is and who he has called you to be—in him. Our worship is so crucial to God that the condition of our heart matters to him. Jesus states in Matthew 5:23-24 that if we come to worship with our gift to him and we remember that our brother or sister has something against us, we are to leave our gift there at the altar and go reconcile with them. *Then* we are to come back and offer our gift to God.

Our ultimate "gift" to God IS our worship. And true worship comes from our heart. Our worship is not just between God and us but also between others and us. This is worshiping God "in spirit and in truth." True worship causes one to submit his or her entire being to God—for God requires nothing less than the giving of one's complete self to him. A lawyer once asked Jesus what the greatest commandment was. This was Christ's response in Mark 12:30: "And you shall love the Lord your God with all your heart and with all your soul and with all your mind and with all your strength."

Worship is a spiritual discipline because we must approach God not just with sincerity, but with an intentionality that says, "I come to you, Lord, on the grounds of <u>your</u> truth."

You <u>can</u> learn and grow in the spiritual discipline of worship!

REST

Most of us are in turmoil and conflict about our lives. We spend large portions of our days worrying about our past, present, and future. But Jesus invites us to live our lives without worry. He also reveals that our Heavenly Father watches over us. The Bible also states that God has a Rest for his people.

"So don't worry about these things, saying, 'What will we eat? What will we drink? What will we wear?' These things dominate the thoughts of unbelievers, but your heavenly Father already knows all your needs. Seek the Kingdom of God above all else, and live righteously, and he will give you everything you need. So don't worry about tomorrow, for tomorrow will bring its own worries. Today's trouble is enough for today." – Matthew 6: 31-34 (NLT)

"Take my yoke upon you. Let me teach you, because I am humble and gentle at heart, and you will find rest for your souls." – Matthew 11:29 (NLT)

"What is the price of two sparrows—one copper coin? But not a single sparrow can fall to the ground without your Father knowing it. And the very hairs on your head are all numbered. So don't be afraid; you are more valuable to God than a whole flock of sparrows." – Matthew 10: 29-31 (NLT)

"So there is a special rest still waiting for the people of God. For all who have entered into God's rest have rested from their labors, just as God did after creating the world. So let us do our best to enter that rest. But if we disobey God, as the people of Israel did, we will fall." – Hebrews 4: 9-12 (NLT)

Learning how to rest in God is a spiritual discipline. We have been trained from birth to "make our own luck" through our own decision-making. We have been taught that everything pretty much depends on us. And so, our minds are constantly racing as we try to figure out our dreams, hopes, and destiny. Many of us may not even sleep well due to pursuing our own agendas!

But God already knows what we need before we ask. God already knows what will happen to us before we do. Nothing takes him by surprise. And Romans 8:28 tells us that God works all things out for the good of those who love him. Remember, a discipline is a practice you commit to on a consistent basis. The spiritual discipline of "Resting in God" is a daily practice which begins as soon as you wake up and continues even when you go to sleep.

"Resting in God" is learning to "fellowship" with him. It happens when we deliberately and consistently keep our minds and hearts on God throughout our day, realizing that Jesus is always with us through the indwelling of the Holy Spirit (John 14:16). And if Jesus is with us, then no matter what happens, we are in good hands. Begin to implement the following measures in your own life to help you grow in "Resting in God."

One: Pray when you wake up, (according to Matthew 6:9-13; Luke 11:1-4), commit yourself and your day to God—those things you know you need to do and the unexpected that will inevitably come your way. Confess his daily provision for your needs. Ask God for his leading and wisdom to meet whatever challenges you will face (James 1:5). Ask him to give you "eyes and ears" to see and hear him at work in your life.

Two: Pray and meditate at the middle and end of the day. Bring before the Lord your day's events. Thank him for successes; ask for his peace and strength for those areas that may bring you anxiety (Isaiah 26:3). Confess God's daily provision for your needs.

Three: During your down time and slow moments in between busy ones, tell Jesus "thank you" for all of his blessings to you. Thank him for that very moment. Tell him you love him not just for what he does but for who he is: The Son of Man. King of Kings. Lord of Lords. Savior of the world. Lover of *your* soul.

You <u>can</u> learn and grow in the spiritual discipline of rest!

A FINAL WORD ON SPIRITUAL DISCIPLINES

Growth, in *any* arena, does not come through haphazard fits and starts. Growth comes from intentional consistent action. Remember, *ALL DISCIPLINES WORK BY TAKING THE TIME TO PUT THEM INTO PRACTICE.* Be intentional in drawing closer to Christ, and watch how your life will become rooted in the reality of God's Eternal Presence. All other ground—other than Christ—is ultimately sinking sand.

THE MARK OF THE BEAST

I know that many Christians are either afraid to read the Book of Revelation or don't understand it when they do read it. Any talk of "the mark" or "666" can generate anxiety in some of us and misinformation in others. Even with this being the case, the book of Revelation itself encourages us to read it and seek to understand what must come to pass.

"Blessed is the one who reads aloud the words of this prophecy, and blessed are those who hear it and take to heart what is written in it, because the time is near." **- Revelation 1:3**

The Apostle John was given a number of visions concerning what would happen in the future, while on the prison island of Patmos in 95 A.D. Jesus himself told him to write down everything he experienced in the visions (except in chapter 10:1-4, where John was told NOT to write what he heard). The purpose was so the Church would know what was to come, how life as we know it would end and how to prepare for Christ's return. John penned the book of Revelation almost 2000 years ago!

Much of what John wrote has been misunderstood over the years. This is especially true where it pertains to the creation of a one-world government that is ruled by the Anti-Christ, who has forced the entire population of the earth to pledge their allegiance to him by taking a mark on the hand or forehead. *This article is relevant for believers today because there is currently a growing convergence of technologies around the world which make the implementation of the "mark of the beast" extremely more likely in the very near future than in previous generations.*

The following is not meant to be an exhaustive breakdown on the "mark of the beast" (nor on the book of Revelation). It is meant to provide you with key information to consider, pray about and research.

156

This way, should "the mark" be implemented on the global populace in the future, you will not be caught unawares, but can take appropriate action!

Here are 3 key Scriptures which speak to this subject:

[16] *"And the second beast required all people small and great, rich and poor, free and slave, to receive a mark on their right hand or on their forehead, [17] so that no one could buy or sell unless he had the mark—the name of the beast or the number of its name."* - **Revelation 13: 16-17**

[9] *"And a third angel followed them, calling in a loud voice, "If anyone worships the beast and its image, and receives its mark on his forehead or hand, [10] he too will drink the wine of God's anger, poured undiluted into the cup of His wrath. And he will be tormented in fire and brimstone in the presence of the holy angels and of the Lamb...."* - **Revelation 14:9-10**

[20] *"But the beast was captured, and with him the false prophet who had performed signs on his behalf, by which he deceived those who had the mark of the beast and worshiped its image. Both of them were thrown alive into the fiery lake of burning sulfur."* - **Revelation 19:20**

A NEW WORLD ORDER IS ON THE HORIZON

There is a push to unify the world's economic system. At its heart is the effort to move to a cashless society. Through technology, we are almost there as it is now possible to buy everything without cash, through debit cards, credit cards, and apps on our phones. China and Sweden have virtually eliminated "paper money" from the populace in favor of paying for everything through cell phone apps. India is not far behind. Even in America, there are growing numbers of people who rarely—if ever—use paper currency, in favor of paying for all of their necessities through the use of their phone apps.

But a new technology is currently being developed, tested, and employed in certain sectors of society—all in the name of safety and convenience. This technology is the RFID microchip. The device is about the size of a grain of rice and can be implanted just under the skin. People can use it to lock/unlock their doors, start their cars, access their computers and of course, buy and sell. It will also be able to store all of a person's medical records—in case of an emergency—as well as their passport information. Who knows what else it will be capable of doing as the world becomes increasingly digital.

In fact, this RFID microchip is not "new" technology... it has been in the works for years. *At the time of this writing, over 10,000 people around the world have been implanted. Sweden has been at the forefront of utilizing the RFID implants. Over 3,500 of its citizens already have these implants in their hands. Discussions are underway to implement placing these type of implants in people's heads.*

Currently, some companies already have their employees "chipped." Test persons are utilizing implants in conjunction with new smart home technology. Some nightclubs give chips to party-goers so they don't have to carry cash to pay for drinks. Many pets are already chipped so they can be tracked if they get lost. *(This was part of the "roll-out plan". Get us used to implanting our pets... and we won't think it too strange to start implanting ourselves.)* There is also talk of starting to implant microchips in babies after they are born to thwart kidnapping attempts at hospitals. And of course, groups have discussed using GPS chip technology to track children who are kidnapped or who run away from their home or school. Again, all in the name of safety and convenience.

MEDIA INFLUENCE AND OUR ACCEPTANCE

Why has all this come to be accepted? A primary player is the media we consume. There have been many television shows and movies which present a world where humans and technology become so intertwined that one can no longer tell where the human ends and the technology begins (Transhumanism). And, the creators of our current technology are always striving to be on the cutting edge in order to make reality what was once considered to be science fiction.

There are also talk shows like *Dr. Oz* and BBC1's, *The One Show* which have promoted RFID microchip implants as the "next big thing" which will revolutionize humanity. Soon, the promotion of these implants will be more prevalent in the media. As the news spreads, increasing numbers of people will want to get their own.

At some point, microchip implants will become the accepted norm, much how DVD's overtook VHS tapes. It is coming and there is nothing we can do to stop it. But we can educate ourselves about this new technology, and look at it from a biblical perspective. After implants are introduced to the larger society, it will become accepted by the masses as the primary way to buy, sell, provide medical information, be tracked and move safely through state, government, and international checkpoints. And then later, getting the chip will become tantamount to pledging allegiance to a new world order... and its ruler.

IS THE RFID CHIP "THE MARK"?

Could this microchip implant technology be the beginning of the "mark of the beast"? ***It bears a strong resemblance to it.*** I am a firm believer in advancing technology to improve our everyday lives. However, a line ***must*** be drawn in order to determine how much advancement is too much. That line is necessary when society wants to implant a microchip into the general populace.

The Bible is very clear on this point: DO NOT get the chip implant. Those who do will have pledged their lives to the fallen socio-economic, geo-political world system. Remember, according to the Bible, **Satan** is *behind* the fallen world system. So, in effect, those who take the chip will have pledged their lives to him in the name of safety and convenience. The Bible states that those who receive the "mark of the beast" *cannot and will not* enter God's Kingdom.

This also means that those who choose **not** to get the "mark" will eventually not be able to buy necessities, conduct business and be tracked by the government. They may also not be able to receive medical treatment as well. These individuals could become "enemies of the state."

Before you write all of this off as hysteria or some paranoid conspiracy theory, take a look at our past. In recent history, Americans (and in some cases the world) have given up many privacy rights in favor of safety from terror threats. It's always harder to retrieve rights once they've been given away. We are slowly becoming a police state. Practically everything we do is traceable through the consumer technology we so readily use. So, things are not as far fetched as they might initially appear to be.

BE AWARE OF THE CONNECTION

This is not meant to make you afraid… only aware—so you can begin to prepare for the inevitable. This is coming either in our lifetime or that of our children and grandchildren. On the surface, there seems to be no spiritual connection with taking a "mark" so you can provide for your family and stay safe in an unsafe world. But Scripture is clear—**there IS a spiritual connection.** Once people begin to have microchips implanted in their bodies for this purpose, then it will be easy for the world system to coerce them into doing anything else in the name of a world government that provides safety and convenience for its citizens.

I have had conversations with people where they welcome "the chip" because it makes sense to them, for the reasons I previously listed. I have also had conversations with Christians, who knew nothing about "the chip" nor the "mark of the beast." Then there are Christians who are misinformed about the "mark." Part of this ignorance is because many Christians don't want to read the book of Revelation because they are afraid of the apocalyptic overtones. Finally, other Christians believe the "mark" has nothing to do with technology at all. They say God couldn't care less about technology, but is more concerned with whether we worship on the Sabbath (Saturday) instead of on Sunday. However, if we take the Bible at face value and look at the world technological landscape, there are too many similarities between the two to be mere coincidence.

When will the "mark" be issued? I don't know. But RFID microchip implants are slated to become mainstream within the next several years. The technology and the world's acceptance of it is growing fast. Is the microchip implant in fact **the** Mark of the Beast or the precursor to the "mark?" Some think so. Others are unsure. But given that the implant is designed to stay in the human body for the long term without being removed, it could be very likely.

It is interesting that when our cell phones receive a new software update, new capabilities are unlocked without ever having to change the hardware. These capabilities were already there... just not "turned on yet." What kind of updates will this RFID microchip receive over time? And what features will be unlocked in the future beyond what has already been stated in this article? And what will having this type of hardware under the skin, which emits and receives wireless electromagnetic frequencies, do to a person's body? Will it affect body chemistry or the mind? And as with any digital system, hacking is inevitable. Can the information stored on the microchip be illegally accessed by others? And what will the government "legally" do with the stored information?

These questions need to be considered. The "mark of the beast" could very well become reality in the next 5-10 years. The infrastructure is already in place to move us to a global cashless society. The United Nations has begun working to make sweeping changes to all aspects of global society by 2030. Pay attention to what is happening in the world.

Don't just accept new technology because someone or the media tells you its the "next big thing". Realize how our growing reliance on technology could in fact become our downfall since life becomes increasingly difficult without it. We are being conditioned to go with the flow of mainstream culture and society, which is increasingly global in nature. Many of us are so entrenched in the world system, that we can't even fathom how to live outside of it. But what happens when the populace is required to get this implant? How will you and I respond?

One thing is for sure; when we read Revelation 13, we see the heart of this issue is: WORSHIP. Will we worship God or the devil? Will we pledge our allegiance to God's kingdom or to the devil's empire? The Mark—whether it is a RFID microchip or something more advanced like a digital tatoo—is coming. We must be ready. Read the book of Revelation, as well as the rest of the Bible, for yourself. Place your faith in Jesus Christ and not in the world system. Do not keep your head in the sand on these issues. Your very life—*for all eternity*—will count on it.

THE RAPTURE

(**NOTE:** This article does not exhaust the subject of The Rapture, but seeks to provide the main themes and concerns associated with it in relation to the time of Tribulation.)

There are a number of Scriptures which detail a phenomenon that has been called, *The Rapture*. This is a momentous event when Jesus Christ dramatically calls all who follow him immediately into his presence. Here is what I Thessalonians 4: 13-18 says about it:

"¹³Brothers and sisters, we do not want you to be uninformed about those who sleep in death, so that you do not grieve like the rest of mankind, who have no hope. ¹⁴For we believe that Jesus died and rose again, and so we believe that God will bring with Jesus those who have fallen asleep in him. ¹⁵According to the Lord's word, we tell you that we who are still alive, who are left until the coming of the Lord, will certainly not precede those who have fallen asleep. ¹⁶For the Lord himself will come down from heaven, with a loud command, with the voice of the archangel and with the trumpet call of God, and the dead in Christ will rise first. ¹⁷After that, we who are still alive and are left will be caught up together with them in the clouds to meet the Lord in the air. And so we will be with the Lord forever. ¹⁸Therefore encourage one another with these words."

I Corinthians 15:51-52 says this: *"⁵¹Listen, I tell you a mystery: We will not all sleep, but we will all be changed— ⁵²in a flash, in the twinkling of an eye, at the last trumpet. For the trumpet will sound, the dead will be raised imperishable, and we will be changed."*

This wonderful imagery has served as a strong comfort to countless Christ-followers for almost 2000 years! Ever since Jesus said he was going to prepare a place for us and would one day come back to receive us to himself *(John 14: 1-3)*, we have been looking forward to his appearing *(Titus 2:13)* and to finally "going home" to be with him. At the same time, there are many in the world who scoff at the idea of Christ returning for his followers—citing how the world has continued to go about its business without so much as a hiccup *(2 Peter 3:3-18)*. These people see the notion of the rapture as pure nonsense. However, for those of us who believe the Bible to be true, we look forward to *THAT DAY*, even if we do not know *exactly* when this event will occur *(Matthew 24:36; 1 Thessalonians 5:2)*.

THREE VIEWS ON THE RAPTURE

There are three views, held by various Christian groups, on the timing of the rapture. These views are held in relation to the end-time tribulation period which is to come on the earth and the Second Coming of Jesus Christ. Before we look at these perspectives, let me say there are a number of Scriptures dealing with this subject of the end-times. To gain a basic sense of the end-time tribulation sequence, read Daniel 9:20-27 *(with an emphasis on verse 27)*, Matthew 24: 3-31 *(with an emphasis on verse 15)*; Mark 13:14, 1 Thessalonians 4: 13-18 and 2 Thessalonians 2: 1-12.

These Scriptures speak of the coming of the Anti-Christ to the third temple in Jerusalem. (*Note: Plans are currently being developed in Israel to begin building the third temple at some future date. This is a milestone to watch for, which lets us know we are steadily approaching the fulfillment of Scripture concerning this matter.*) Also, at some point, the world will unite under *ONE* new government and the Anti-Christ will become the leader of *that* government. The Bible reveals that his leadership will take place over a 7 year period. This serves as the backdrop for the rapture.

FIRST VIEW: Some Christian denominations believe the rapture will happen **BEFORE** the Anti-Christ is revealed and the time of tribulation comes on the earth. They are called Pre-tribulationalists. According to this belief, the Church will be raptured away and will be in heaven with Christ as the world endures the Great Tribulation. Revelation 3:10 is one scripture that is used to support this belief. Here, Christ speaks to the Church in Philadelphia:

"¹⁰Since you have kept my command to endure patiently, I will also keep you from the hour of trial that is going to come on the whole world to test the inhabitants of the earth."

SECOND VIEW: Other Christian groups believe the rapture will happen at some point **DURING** the 7 year period. They are called Mid-tribulationalists. This 7 year period is divided into two parts—each being 3.5 years long. Mid-tribulationalists believe Christians will experience the first half, but will be raptured to heaven before the severe outpouring of God's wrath during the second half. This means they will see the Anti-Christ revealed to the world.

THIRD VIEW: Still, other Christian groups believe the rapture will happen towards **THE END** of the tribulation. They are called Post-tribulationalists. They believe many Christians will experience the full 7 years *(utopia for the first half and tribulation in the second)* along with the world as the wrath of the Anti-Christ is poured out on those who refuse to pledge their allegiance to him.

A scripture passage often used to support the second and third view is Matthew 24: 37-41. Here, Jesus states:

"37As it was in the days of Noah, so it will be at the coming of the Son of Man. 38For in the days before the flood, people were eating and drinking, marrying and giving in marriage, up to the day Noah entered the ark; 39and they knew nothing about what would happen until the flood came and took them all away. That is how it will be at the coming of the Son of Man. 40Two men will be in the field; one will be taken and the other left. 41Two women will be grinding with a hand mill; one will be taken and the other left."

What has been said about this scripture passage in reference to the timing of the rapture is that, while God used the ark to rescue Noah (his family and the animals) *from* the flood, Noah still had to go **through** the flood—although God protected him.

AN OBSERVATION

I have been a Christian for over 30 years and have visited numerous churches in America. Some of the denominations have been Evangelical in nature and others have not. (Baptist, Methodist, Lutheran, Presbyterian, Pentecostal, Apostolic, Church of God, 7th Day Adventist, and Non-denominational.) During my college years until now, I have noticed a trend for many Christians in America: *we don't like to suffer.* As a result of this preference, many like to believe in the *first* view of the rapture.

Jesus will come and get us <u>before</u> the Anti-Christ is revealed and the time of great suffering comes to the inhabitants of the earth.

What I have found is that many have **PLACED THEIR FAITH IN THIS VIEW MORE THAN IN JESUS.** What does this mean? If Jesus does not rapture us before the Anti-Christ is revealed and the tribulation begins, than our faith in God will fall apart and disintegrate.

Now, I don't know about you, but I do not want to go through the tribulation. I don't like to suffer, nor do I know anyone who would willingly volunteer to suffer. Yet, Scripture tells us we can't know the day nor the hour that Christ will return to get us. *(Over the years, many have tried to figure it out and failed miserably.)* But Christ's return could be at **any** point. It could happen before you finish this book! Or it can be at any other point in the future. Either way, the Bible admonishes us to steadily look for and be ready for Christ's appearing.

In addition to this, the Bible also talks about there being a great falling away (Apostasy) of those who profess to believe in Jesus before he returns *(2 Thessalonians 2:1-5).* I can't help but wonder if *part* of that "falling away" will have to do with those who placed their faith in the rapture rather than in Jesus? Just think about it. How many people do you know—today— who have given up on a relationship with God because he didn't respond according to their time schedule or things didn't work out how they expected? What would happen if the timing of the rapture doesn't meet our own expectations and we have to endure some form of suffering for our faith?

WHAT DOES "REVEALED" MEAN?

Take a look at 2 Thessalonians 2:1-10:

¹Concerning the coming of our Lord Jesus Christ and our being gathered to him, we ask you, brothers and sisters, ²not to become easily unsettled or alarmed by the teaching allegedly from us—whether by a prophecy or by word of mouth or by letter—asserting that the day of the Lord has already come.

³Don't let anyone deceive you in any way, for that day will not come until the rebellion occurs and the man of lawlessness is revealed, the man doomed to destruction. ⁴He will oppose and will exalt himself over everything that is called God or is worshiped, so that he sets himself up in God's temple, proclaiming himself to be God. ⁵Don't you remember that when I was with you I used to tell you these things? ⁶And now you know what is holding him back, so that he may be revealed at the proper time. ⁷For the secret power of lawlessness is already at work; but the one who now holds it back will continue to do so till he is taken out of the way. ⁸And then the lawless one will be revealed, whom the Lord Jesus will overthrow with the breath of his mouth and destroy by the splendor of his coming. ⁹The coming of the lawless one will be in accordance with how Satan works. He will use all sorts of displays of power through signs and wonders that serve the lie, ¹⁰and all the ways that wickedness deceives those who are perishing. They perish because they refused to love the truth and so be saved."

The "lawless one" is the Anti-Christ who, according to verse 9, will be directed by Satan himself. This person must be revealed at his appointed time. Currently, according to verses 6 and 7, there is something holding the lawless one at bay, which must be removed before he can be revealed. It is the Holy Spirit who is holding things at bay. Now, where does the Holy Spirit dwell on earth? According to 1 Corinthians 6:19, the Holy Spirit dwells in each believer-follower of Jesus Christ. So, it stands to reason that the Holy Spirit will be removed from the earth when all believer-followers of Jesus have been raptured from the earth. After all, it does say in 1 Thessalonians 5:9, *"For God did not appoint us to suffer wrath but to receive salvation through our Lord Jesus Christ."*

The issue, however, is with the word "revealed" in verses 3, 6, 8. The word in the Greek is: Apokalypto. It means *to be disclosed, plainly signified, distinctly declared, to be set forth, announced, to be discovered in true character, to be manifested, to appear.* The question is *when* will the Anti-Christ be revealed? Does "revealed" mean that the rapture will happen just before this person takes the stage as the leader of the one world government? *(So that we who follow Christ won't be around to see this happen).* Or does "revealed" have a more nuanced meaning? Since the word means *to be discovered in true character,* the scenario could be more like this:

166

At the beginnig of the 7 year Tribulation period, the one world government takes shape out of the crucible of some global catastrophe and a leader rises to lead it. The world is enamored by this person's charismatic personality, his impeccable credentials and his ability to bring peace and prosperity to a desperate global populace. War and poverty are eradicated as he helms a successful peace treaty in the Middle East. Israel is enpowered to build a third temple on the Temple Mount and reinstates its relgious sacrificial system.

This leader is able to connect with all classes of people as he paints a vision of a new dawn for humanity, where all of our differences are transcended and untapped potential can finally be realized. For three and a half years, he moves the world forward towards great technological and humanitarian exploits. Personal freedoms are willingly sacrificed to the one world government in the name of security, efficiency and harmony as humanity unites in a way not seen since the Tower of Babel. And those who speak out against him—especially Christians and Jews—are persecuted and seen as enemies of the state.

It seems this leader can do no wrong as his approval ratings are the highest of any leader past or present. However, towards the end of the three-and-a-half years... cracks in his facade begin to appear. Then the rapture happens— believer-followers of Christ are whisked away from the earth—**and the true nature of this leader's character is revealed** as he enters the most holy place of Jerusalem's third temple and declares himself to be exalted above God. Then, the Great Tribulation begins as he morphs into a terror, the likes of which the inhabitants of the earth have never seen. At the same time, God pours out his wrath on the unbelieving inhabitants of earth.

THE BOTTOM LINE FOR CHRIST-FOLLOWERS

Which scenario is more likely? That believer-followers of Christ are raptured before the Anti-Christ appears on the world stage? Or that we are raptured before the Anti-Christ reveals his true nature and character to the world? We do not know. Scripture does not *specifically* tell us. However, the bottom line for us as believer-followers of Jesus Christ has to be this: **faithfulness to Jesus regardless of the timing of his return.** While no one wants to suffer, do not place your faith in not having to suffer for Christ's sake. **Place your faith in Jesus Christ alone—no matter what may come in the future.** To do anything other than this is to set ourselves up for the possibility of deception and failure.

I don't know when Christ will return to receive us to himself. But I know he promised that he would, and the signs of the times are increasing all around us! Jesus is our bridegroom from Matthew 25:1-13! Sadly, the church has been asleep—dreaming of our own earthly kingdoms—oblivious to the truth that our bridegroom is *actually* coming. But the call is being declared: "Here is the bridegroom! Come out to meet him!" We are waking up and trimming our lamps, but may we be wise like those bridesmaids who brought extra oil with them. May we fill ourselves with the oil of God's Holy Spirit. This way, we will be ready for him who loves us, and we will enter the marriage celebration of the Lamb!

If the rapture happens before the Anti-Christ comes and the tribulation begins, then wonderul! If it happens during the half-way point, right before God pours out his wrath on an unbelieving world, then hallelujah! If it happens at the end of the great tribulation, then LORD, please give us the ability to endure faithfully to the end! Since I can't know the exact time, *I won't place my faith in the timing.* **I will place my faith in Jesus Christ himself—and trust he has my future under control.**

Whether I die and find myself standing in his presence or am alive when he parts the sky to rapture his Church, I just want to be ready—whenever the time comes. I hope you will be ready as well. *That* is the bottom line. Let us remember Jesus' words in Matthew 24:13:

"BUT THE ONE WHO ENDURES AND BEARS UP [UNDER SUFFERING] TO THE END WILL BE SAVED." (Amplified)

However our end comes... may God get the glory out of our lives. And may we remember what Romans 8:18 says: **"...*our present sufferings are not worth comparing with the glory that will be revealed in us.*"** That glory will be revealed when Jesus calls us home to him! Maranatha! *(Come, Lord Jesus... COME)!*

YOUR KINGDOM COME!

CHRIST'S MILLENNIAL REIGN

*"And I saw an angel coming down out of heaven, having the key to the Abyss and holding in his hand a great chain. **2** He seized the dragon, that ancient serpent, who is the devil, or Satan, and bound him for a thousand years. **3** He threw him into the Abyss, and locked and sealed it over him, to keep him from deceiving the nations anymore until the thousand years were ended. After that, he must be set free for a short time. **4** I saw thrones on which were seated those who had been given authority to judge. And I saw the souls of those who had been beheaded because of their testimony about Jesus and because of the word of God. They had not worshiped the beast or its image and had not received its mark on their foreheads or their hands. They came to life and reigned with Christ a thousand years. **5** (The rest of the dead did not come to life until the thousand years were ended.) This is the first resurrection. **6** Blessed and holy are those who share in the first resurrection. The second death has no power over them, but they will be priests of God and of Christ and will reign with him for a thousand years."* —**Revelation 20:1-6**

Reading Revelation 20 raises several questions about the 1000 years (known as Christ's Millennial Reign). Two such questions are: why would Jesus choose to imprison Satan for a thousand years only to have him released to cause chaos? Why would Jesus not just simply vanquish Satan at his second coming? I will admit that not understanding these and other questions caused me to gloss over this major biblical event. I relegated the thousand year reign to the category of a "minor footnote" when compared to the eternity that awaits thereafter. As a result, I did not seek to gain greater understanding before publishing the *first edition* of Resurrection.

However, after the book was released, I began to unexpectedly encounter passage-after-passage in the Bible relating to Christ's thousand year reign. As time passed and my understanding grew, the Holy Spirit began to impress upon me the need to release a *second edition* which included this subject. I praise God for his grace, mercy and patience! So, let's take a look at the coming Millennial Reign.

Scripture is clear: Jesus Christ will return to earth at a future point in human history. This is called his 2nd Coming. At his 1st Coming, Jesus came quietly as a baby... arriving on earth under the radar of rulers both human and demonic. He was the Passover Lamb of God who came to take away the sin of the world. He sacrificed himself on the cross to secure salvation for humanity. He then rose from the dead with all power so that we too will rise in power on the last day. Forty days after his resurrection, Jesus ascended back to heaven to prepare a place for all who surrender their hearts to him. He promised to return one day to receive us to himself. He also promised to return at the conclusion of this Age. What will he do when he returns?

When Jesus comes the second time, all the world will see him *(Rev. 19:11-21)*. He will arrive as the King of Kings and Lord of Lords. He will be the Lion of the Tribe of Judah! When he returns, he will fulfill the prayer that he taught his disciples to pray some 2000 years ago. The prayer all who follow him have prayed ever since. "Our Father in heaven, hallowed be your name, your kingdom come, your will be done, on earth as it is in heaven..."

When Jesus returns with the armies of heaven he will set up his kingdom on earth for a thousand years. Revelation 20:1-3 reveals that a powerful angel will imprison Satan in the Abyss! He will be bound in darkness—unable to deceive the nations of the earth for 1000 years. Over the years, people have studied and debated whether this is a literal or figurative thousand years. I believe when you read all relevant verses of Scripture pertaining to this issue the conclusion is both clear and staggering. In between time and eternity Jesus will literally reign for 1000 years! Here is an overview of what the Old and New Testaments tell us:

Christ's reign will begin with him setting down on the Mount of Olives in Jerusalem. The people of Israel will then acknowledge Jesus Christ as "The Son of Man" found in Daniel 7—their long-awaited Messiah and Savior of the world. They will weep bitterly at the realization of their previous rejection as they then surrender to his lordship. Jesus will resurrect and reward those who lost their lives for his sake during the time of world-wide Tribulation which takes place just before his return. Then all who belong to him—blessed by his Father—will inherit the kingdom prepared for them since the creation of the world *(Matthew 25:34)* and they will rule with him. The nations of the world will be brought before Christ in the valley of Jehosophat to give an account of how they treated the Jews—his chosen people. Jesus will then begin to restore the kingdom to Israel. In doing so, he will fulfill every promise made to Abraham.

Jesus will have dominion over the entire earth and will rule from Jerusalem—seated on the throne of David. He will also establish what had been impossible before that moment: world peace. The inhabitants of the earth will rally around him as he begins to restore this broken planet. The citizens of his kingdom will work with him to restore the earth and represent his rulership. For 1000 years, Jesus will demonstrate true and righteous government. The people of the world will learn of him, will work and create to his glory and will be prepared for eternity. Lifespans will increase. The truths revealed will be unparalleled. The stories told by billions upon billions of redeemed resurrected saints will be amazing. But the Greatest Story ever told will be shared by Jesus himself as he explains God's plan of salvation and what is to come!

Not only will earth's inhabitants be at peace, no longer warring with one another, but creation itself will also be at peace. Wild animals will no longer pose a threat to human life. Poisonous creatures will no longer be feared. "The wolf will live with the lamb, the leopard will lie down with the goat, the calf and the lion and the yearling together; and a little child will lead them" *(Isaiah 11:6)*. Men and women will no longer work the ground by the sweat of their brow. Weather and sea will no longer rage out of control. The earth will be filled with the knowledge of the glory of the Lord as the waters cover the sea" *(Habakkuk 2:14)*.

The Millennial Reign will be glorious. However, a final conflict will arise when the thousand years is complete. Satan will be released from the Abyss and will make one last attempt to overthrow God's sovereignty. His scheme will prove futile and he will be cast into the lake of fire to suffer in torment forever. Then all humans who have denied God throughout the generations will be physically resurrected. They will stand before Christ for final judgment at the great white throne. Their end will be the same as the devil's... they will be cast into the eternal fires created for the devil and his angels *(Matthew 25:41)*. The lake of fire is called the second death.

Again, the Bible does not provide a direct answer to the question, "**Why** does Jesus allow Satan to be imprisoned in the Abyss instead of immediately destroying him?" Revelation 20:3b simply states, *"After that [the thousand years], he [Satan] must be set free for a short time."* Verses 7 and 8 tells us, *"When the thousand years are over, Satan will be released from his prison 8 and will go out to deceive the nations in the four corners of the earth—God and Magog—and to gather them for battle. In number they are like the sand on the seashore."*

What **can** be infered from the totality of Scripture is that Satan has always tried to make the claim that people only follow God because of his blessings. That if allowed, he could get humans to "curse God to his face." (*We see this in the book of Job in the Old Testament where God allowed the devil to attack his righteous servant*). In Genesis 3 we also see that he tries to claim that God is not being truthful with humanity... that God can't be trusted and is not truly good. Scriture also infers that Satan and his fallen angels rebelled against God with their eyes wide open. Meaning: they knew he was the Source of all life and Creator of all things.

Apparently, at Christ's 2nd Coming and during his Millennial Reign, those humans who are still alive (unbelievers) will be given a similar opportunity and test. No longer will they be able to profess, "where's the evidence that God exists?" They will see him clearly. The truth will be fully evident for all to comprehend. They will serve under his governing leadership. They will see his blessings and have the chance to receive answers to their most pressing questions. They will *live long and prosper.*

Then, at the end of 1000 years under Jesus' righteous rulership, they will face the final test of their allegience: Satan will be released from his prison. And sadly, many who will have experienced God's goodness will still choose to side with the devil. They will try to destroy God's people in Jerusalem and will face utter annihilation instead. Why is Satan always after Jerusalem and God's people? Because they are a constant reminder of God's sovereign plan of salvation. They also reinforce the fact that Satan and his fallen angels can never be redeemed because they rebelled against God knowing full well what they were doing! However, just before Jesus died in our place, he declared, "Father forgive them [us] for they don't know what they are doing!" We didn't have the full picture, but rather were manipulated by evil.

Why is Satan allowed to cause chaos after the 1000 year reign? Perhaps so his claim, that God is unjust, can be completely and totally disproven! In the end, no one will be able to say that God is unfair in his judgments. There will be no excuse for refusing to follow Jesus Christ who sacrificed his own life to save us from the second death—the eternal fires created as punishment for the devil and his fallen angels.

There are many Old and New Testament Scriptures which provide a framework for us to imagine what the Millennial Reign of Christ will be like. I have listed several below. May they aid you in your journey to discover the truth about what God is up to in the world and your place in it. I also pray these passages will provide you with hope to face the future knowing that everything changes at Christ's 2nd coming!

Additional Scripture References: Genesis 12:1-3; 15:1-21; Psalm 86:9; Isaiah 2:1-5; 9:6-7; 11:1-10; 25:6-8; 65:17-25; Daniel 7; Joel 3; Zechariah 12:10; 14:3-9; Matthew 19:27-29; 24:26-51; 25:31-46; Luke 19:17; 22:28-30; Acts 1:6-11; Revelation 1:1-8; 20:7-15

BONUS THOUGHT: As wonderful as the Millennial Reign will be... Chapters 21 and 22 of Revelation reveals that God has an even greater, more expansive and amazing reality awaiting those who have been redeemed. This will come *after* Satan and all who have sided with him are judged; *after* all sin, death and evil has been eradicated. It is then that God remakes the universe and marries heaven and earth together in a way that is beyond our current ability to comprehend! And we, who belong to him, will be present to watch him create this new universe! And then we will participate with him in whatever he has planned for eternity!

WHY DID JESUS COME?

Followers of Jesus sometimes have difficulty articulating the gospel and explaining why Jesus Christ came to earth. If we don't have an understanding for ourselves, it will be hard to grow in our faith and also to share our faith with others. Here are 6 reasons why Jesus Christ came to redeem those who would believe. Examine the Scriptures for yourself!

ONE: *TO DO HIS FATHER'S WILL:*
John 6:38-39; John 17:4; Hebrews 2:8; Isaiah 53:10-11

TWO: *TO SEEK AND SAVE THE LOST:*
Mark 10:45; Luke 19:10; 5:31-32; John 3:16; 14:6; Acts 4:12; Galatians 4:4-5

THREE: *TO DESTROY THE WORKS OF THE DEVIL:*
Genesis 3:14-15; Hebrews 2:14-15; 1 John 3:8

FOUR: *TO BE EXALTED AND GLORIFIED BY THE FATHER:*
John 8:50; John 17:5; Philippians 2:9-11

FIVE: *TO BECOME THE FIRSTBORN AMONG MANY BROTHERS AND SISTERS:* *Romans 8:29; Hebrews 2:1-18*

SIX: *TO GIVE US THE VICTORY OVER DEATH:*
Romans 8:37; 1 Corinthians 15: 54-57

An Invitation to the Seeker

I don't want to assume that if you are reading these words, you are already a believer in Jesus Christ. Perhaps you are... maybe you are not.

If you have not already given your life to Jesus, I have good news! You can do it now. And it is not complicated. If you read this book, then you already know Jesus did the complicated work in order to give you and I the opportunity to receive his salvation. And he gives us the path, in the Bible, that we each must go down if we want to belong to him. Here it is. If you feel God tugging at your heart and you want to give him your life, read what the Bible declares in Romans 10: 9-11:

⁹If you declare with your mouth, "Jesus is Lord," and believe in your heart that God raised him from the dead, you will be saved. ¹⁰For it is with your heart that you believe and are justified, and it is with your mouth that you profess your faith and are saved. ¹¹As Scripture says, "Anyone who believes in him will never be put to shame."

God knows the condition of your heart and the thoughts of your mind. And when you call out to him, he takes notice and responds. Do you believe that Jesus is Lord—that he is God's Son and ruler of all? Do you believe that he died on the cross, in your place, to forgive your sins? Do you believe God, the Father raised him from the dead on the 3rd day?

Then confess that belief with your mouth—out loud. Admit to Jesus that you are a sinner and you can't save yourself. Tell Jesus that you need him to save you and bring you into a right relationship with his heavenly Father. Ask him to forgive your sins and to wash you clean with his blood which he shed on the cross for you. Commit your life and destiny into his hands.

According to the scripture above, if you have just done this, then you are now saved! You are now born again! You are now a child of God! According to Luke 15: 7, 10 all of heaven rejoices at your salvation! Now, as God's child, he wants you to grow in the knowledge of who he is and who you are in him. Here are 2 things you can do to help you grow.

ONE: Read the gospel of John in the Bible. **TWO:** Ask God to lead you to a Bible-believing church, where you can get plugged into a community of Christ-followers.

Finally, walking with the Lord Jesus Christ is not a sprint. It's not cross-country. It's not even a marathon nor is it a triathlon (although it may encompass elements of each). This walk with Christ is daily and it is life long. You will have wonderful exhilarating moments! You will also encounter challenges, obstacles and opposition. However, through it all, Jesus promises to be with you and to never leave you alone—<u>especially</u> during those times when you *feel* all alone. Those are when he is the closest. (Counter intuitive I know...).

This Christ-following walk was never meant to be done in our own strength. Always ask for Jesus to lead, guide and strengthen you through his Holy Spirit and he will. And one day, you and I will meet... if not in this life on earth, then surely at the Resurrection!

An Invitation to the Christian

I don't want to assume that if you are reading these words that you are a believer in Christ who is on fire for God and experiencing the fullness of his Presence in your life.

If I have learned anything in the 30+ years of walking with Jesus, it's that God is inexhaustible! In other words, there is always more to learn! You never "arrive" and the "length" of time you have been a Christian doesn't necessarily determine your level of spiritual growth, if the quality of the time with Jesus has been spotty at best.

Our Heavenly Father has unfolding levels of truth he wants to reveal to each of us who belong to him. <u>This truth concerns his Son</u>. There are higher heights to climb with Christ! There are greater depths to search, farther lengths to run, and wider expanses to journey with Christ! This relationship with Jesus is an unfolding mystery of discovery!

Several months into the Covid-19 pandemic, the Lord helped me understand the major title he used to reveal himself in the gospels: **The Son of Man**. Did you know he used this title 78 times to refer to himself? Messiah/Christ is used 49 times. Son of God is used 25 times. And Son of David is used 14 times. These other titles are used mostly by others *about* Jesus. He uses them sparingly. But, Jesus used the title, "*The Son of Man" often* to refer to himself!

Why is this significant? Because every time Jesus uses this title in the gospels, to refer to himself, he is pointing people directly to Daniel 7. In this chapter, the Son of Man is revealed as being divine! He receives an eternal kingdom from the Ancient of Days! In this one vision the prophet Daniel sees God the Father and God the Son! So, 78 times in the gospels, Jesus is saying to the people [and to us], **"I am God in the flesh!"**

This realization has changed how I read the gospels! Hopefully, it will change how you read them as well! The things Jesus says and does now make more sense within this context! What also amazed me was that this truth was present in the text all along! But God had to open my eyes to see it...

The temptation we face is that we would reach a certain level and then "pitch our tent there and build our house." The fear is that we become comfortable at a particular level and would rather not continue the journey of discovery with Christ.

Jesus tells us, "Follow Me." And while he is the Good Shepherd who "makes us to lie down in green pastures," a shepherd doesn't stay in one place forever. The shepherd leads the sheep to a particular set of destinations! The danger is this: we make our place at one level, but when Jesus walks on ahead, we are so entrenched in the world we've created for ourselves, that we refuse to keep following our Shepherd!

<u>So, this is an invitation to you: keep following the Good Shepherd who is The Son of Man!</u> Wherever he leads you, keep growing in Christ! Do not allow yourself to become stagnant. Keep seeking his face! Keep eating and digesting his Word! Keep allowing him to lead you out of your comfort zones, so that he can truly make you into the person he desires you to be.

THAT person is a lover of Jesus who is fully confident in Christ's ability to lead and provide for you at all times, no matter the circumstance. Because, as your faith grows, so does your availability and obedience to God. And when a person is fully available to Christ, then anything is possible! May this book cause you to follow Christ with a renewed passion, focus and vigor from now into eternity!

[20]*He [Jesus] replied, "Because you have so little faith. Truly I tell you, if you have faith as small as a mustard seed, you can say to this mountain, 'Move from here to there,' and it will move. Nothing will be impossible for you"* (Matthew 17:20).

<u>This is an invitation from Christ to you. There is more to experience on your Christian journey!</u> *(For more information on Jesus as The Son of Man, read the book, Son of Man: The Gospel of Daniel 7, by Samuel Whitefield.)*

Acknowledgments

I want to say thank you to the following people for their valuable assistance with this book. To my wife, Ijnanya for listening to each page and idea associated with this project. To my father, the Rev. Dr. Allen Paul Weaver Jr, for proofing this manuscript for overall theological accuracy. To my friend and brother in the Lord, Joeffrey Gardner for reading this from a 'layman' point of view. To my editor on this project, the amazing Dorette Saunders! You truly helped to make a good thing better!

About the Author

Rev. Allen Paul Weaver III is the author of several books which help readers overcome the obstacles to their God-given dreams and purpose.

His previously published works include **Transition: Breaking Through the Barriers** (autobiographical anthology), **MOVE! Your Destiny is Waiting on You** (personal development), the epic **Speedsuit Powers Trilogy** (young adult fiction) and its follow-up, **Flight** (young adult fiction). He has also published the followup to this book, **The Resurrection Life: *A 40 Day Journey with Jesus*** (devotional). He is currently working on additional manuscripts for future publication.

Allen earned his bachelors degree in Speech/Mass Communications from Bethune-Cookman University. He earned his master's of divinity degree in theology from Colgate Rochester Crozer Divinity School.

He has been preaching and teaching God's Word in a variety of church and conference settings for over twenty years. Through preaching, teaching, writing and other gifts, Allen seeks to help people discover their true identity in Christ.

Allen and his wonderful wife, Ijnanya have one amazing son.

Visit www.APW3.com to learn more.

What Now?

You have just read **Resurrection**! I hope you enjoyed it and that it helped open your understanding to the Grand Narrative of the Bible. The question is: *what do you do now?* We often read books, gain knowledge and move on to other things in life. But in order for us to benefit from the knowledge, we have to put it into some kind of meaningful action.

How do you continue to build upon this foundation so that you can grow closer to Christ? How do you dive deeper into God's Word? How can you use what you've learned to have a positive impact on others?

Here are several suggestions to help you move forward. I have placed them within two categories: *Spiritually* and *Socially*.

SPIRITUALLY

ONE: Seek Christ about your next steps. He may have a specific and unexpected assignment for you to do.

TWO: Make sure you read all of the articles in the appendix section, even if you feel like you already know the subject matter. You never know what "aha" moments may arise as you do.

THREE: Study the Scripture passages mentioned in the appendix. This will help you to "connect the dots" of Scripture to better grasp God's Grand Narrative.

FOUR: Journal about your reading experience—the insights the Lord has shown you, how they have helped your understanding of Scripture, and have impacted your day-to-day interactions with others.

FIVE: Read **Resurrection** again. It will help to reinforce your understanding and you may even see something new!

SOCIALLY

ONE: Tell others about this book! If **Resurrection** has been a blessing to you, let others know! Word of mouth is still, hands down, the best form of advertising. Please use whatever platform that is available to you to help spread the word. (phone, text, email, Facebook, etc)

TWO: Consider purchasing copies for family, friends, co-workers *(and even your enemies)*. Knowledge is truly a gift which keeps on giving. And the greatest form of knowledge any of us can have is about God's love demonstrated through Jesus. The benefits last for eternity!

THREE: Start a book club where you can read **Resurrection** with others and discuss it together. The experience of a group gathering together in a relaxed atmosphere (whether in person or virtually) to discuss a book in detail is invaluable!

FOUR: Let me know how this book has impacted you. Writing and publishing a book is often a one-way phenomenon. Authors do not always get a sense of how their books are impacting readers. Feel free to contact me through my website, APW3.com, and share your thoughts, questions and concerns.

FIVE: Leave a review on amazon.com. Many people read reviews in order to determine whether or not they will purchase a book or other product. Your review can help someone else—you may never meet—to make a decision to buy **Resurrection**. And that decision could help change their life forever! Also, the more reviews a book gets on amazon.com the greater exposure it receives so more people will learn about it.

Again, thank you for considering all of these ways to increase your engagement with this book. You are holding in your hands one of the most important books that I have written to date. The other is my new book, **The Resurrection Life: A 40 Day Journey with Jesus.**

I believe these books can help all of us—as believers in Christ—to grow in our knowledge and understanding of God's Word, enabling us to have an intimate relationship with Jesus—who is the Son of Man of

Daniel 7. I also believe these books can help us become better witnesses for Christ as his 2nd Coming draws ever closer.

May God bless you, keep you and guide you each day, for his glory, for your good and the good of those around you. In Jesus' Name… Amen.

—Rev. Allen Paul Weaver III, M.Div

READ THE NEXT BOOK IN THE SERIES:

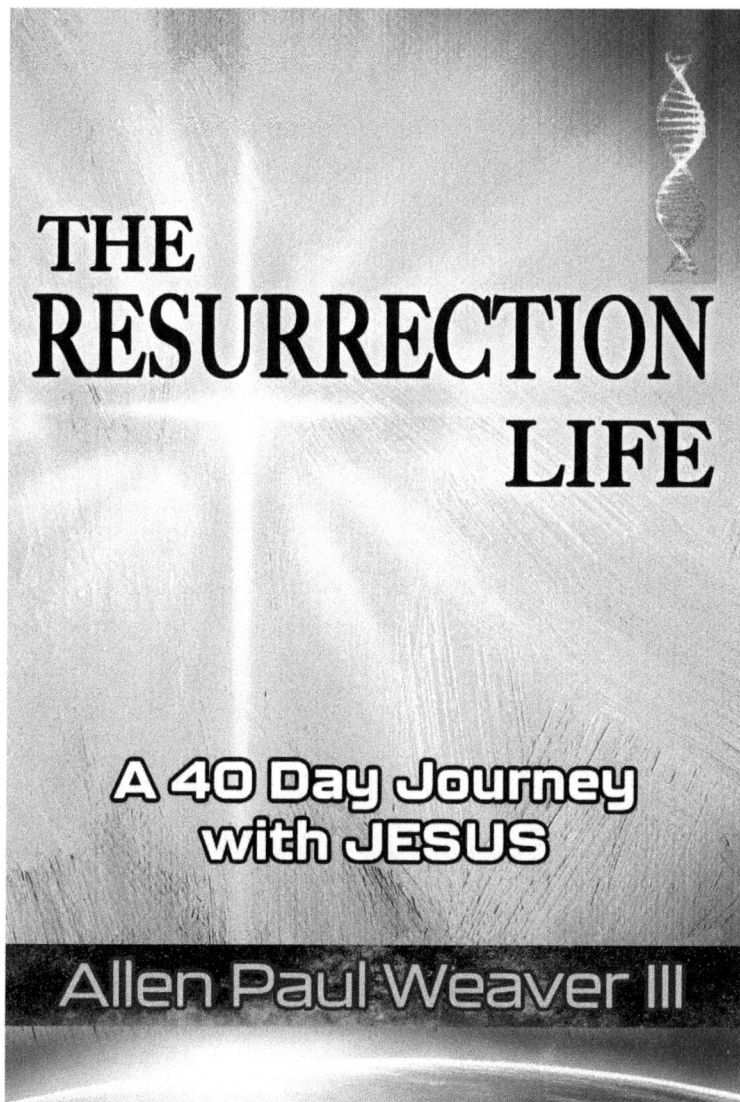

THE
RESURRECTION
LIFE

A 40 Day Journey
with JESUS

Allen Paul Weaver III

www.ingramcontent.com/pod-product-compliance
Lightning Source LLC
Chambersburg PA
CBHW071529040426
42452CB00008B/936